TOUGH TIMES NEVER LAST

7 SECRETS TO OVERCOMING TOUGH TIMES

Bishop Dr. Emmanuel MacJones

TOUGH TIMES NEVER LAST
7 Secrets To Overcoming Tough Times

by Bishop Dr. Emmanuel MacJones

Printed in the United States of America.

ISBN 9781498482165

PUBLISHED & PRODUCED BY: NABERM PUBLICATION
P.O BOX 4222 Scranton
P. A 18505

Editors: Dr. KINGSLEY VAN DER PUIJE
SONNY VANDERPUYE
KADMIEL VANDERPUIJE

PRINTED BY: EMJ PUBLISHING
10125 Colesville Rd.
Suite 3157 Silver Spring, MD 20901
bishopmacjones@gmail.com
Tel: (703) 898 2111 or (202) 697-1408

www.xulonpress.com

TABLE OF CONTENTS

Preface: Why I Wrote This Book vii
Dedication ix
Acknowledgments xi
Introduction. xiii

Chapter 1: What Are Tough Times 15
Chapter 2: Why The Tough Times? 37
Chapter 3: Examples Of Tough Times In The Bible 68
Chapter 4: What Not To Do In Tough Times. 120
Chapter 5: How To Overcome Tough Times – The Way Out. 171
Chapter 6: 7 Secrets To Overcoming Tough Times . . .214
Chapter 7: Secret #1–Wisdom. 228
Chapter 8: Secret #2–Planning 239
Chapter 9: Secret #3–Partnership And Networking . .244
Chapter 10: Secret #4–Faith. .266
Chapter 11: Secret #5–Change 273
Chapter 12: Secret #6–Obedience. 277
Chapter 13: Secret # 7 – Problem Solving/Service 284
Chapter 14: Never Give Up. 295
Chapter 15: Now, Overcome Tough Times 298
Chapter 16: My Story For His Glory. 300
Chapter 17: How You Can Know God's Love 302

About The Author 313

PREFACE

Why I Wrote this Book

When you look at the bombardment from the television, radio, and newspapers, all you see and hear are the reports of the doom and gloom and tough times that are coming on the nations and the globe.

We are in tough times, but there is a way out. God has planned that in every situation that will affect planet earth, His people will be covered. Seeing the distress and disaster facing nations and hearing all the negative talk, and bloodshed, I felt led by God to speak out against the fear that is being preached from the media and to remind God's people that tough times never last. This is not the first time for tough times; neither will it be the last time for tough times to happen. The good news is this, there are secrets to follow and apply in all tough times that will bring the best out of you and make you a victor and not a victim according to I John 5:1-5

I wrote this book in order to put into your hands the seven secrets God gave me for our nations and generations. In Genesis 41, we see very clearly that God raised Joseph up to lead the Israelites and Egyptians out of their tough times by giving him secrets. The people obeyed him and overcame the tough times. These secrets work. Obey them and believe them and you too will come out victorious over your tough times. This is the end of your tough times. See you at the top!

DEDICATION

This book is lovingly dedicated to The Most High God; the Kings of kings, the Lord of lords, the Father of us all, for His mercy and compassion; He picked me, as a no body and made somebody out of me, to Him be praise forever. I AM THAT I AM; I bless Your Name. Thank You for the training, understanding, and for pulling me through tough times. You are my Jehovah Jireh, Jehovah Shamah, and Defender. PSALM 27

The Lord is my light and my salvation; whom shall I fear? The LORD is the strength of my life; of whom shall I be afraid?

1. When the wicked, even mine enemies and my foes, came upon me to eat up my flesh, they stumbled and fell.

2. Though an host should encamp against me, my heart shall not fear: though war should rise against me, in this will I be confident.
3. One thing have I desired of the LORD, that will I seek after; that I may dwell in the house of the LORD all the days of my life, to behold the beauty of the LORD, and to enquire in his temple.
4. For in the time of trouble he shall hide me in his pavilion: in the secret of his tabernacle shall he hide me; he shall set me up upon a rock.
5. And now shall mine head be lifted up above mine enemies round about me: therefore will I offer in his tabernacle sacrifices of joy; I will sing, yea, I will sing praises unto the LORD. Thank You Lord!!!

ACKNOWLEDGMENTS

My heartfelt thanks and praise go to Almighty God, our Father, the giver of all gifts, Who has given me the gift of writing. The Holy Scriptures tell us in James 1:17 that ***"every good gift and every perfect gift is from above, and cometh down from the Father of lights, with whom is no variableness, neither shadow of turning."*** My profound thanks and praise also go to the Holy Spirit, my teacher, Who teaches me what to write and how to write it. Without them, there would not be a book.

My deepest appreciation and gratitude also go to my Beloved Savior, Jesus Christ, for saving my soul and who has enrolled me into His army to teach and disciple souls for Him through writing.

My appreciation also goes to the best team on earth, who worked so hard and painfully to make this work a reality; Dr. Kingsley Van Der Puije, Joseph Sonny Vanderpuye, Kadmiel Van Der Puije, Evangelist Mary Faith Gandire, Rev.Young and Minister Woods Jackyline – I say thank you. Expect your rewards.

To my beloved wife, Bishop Mrs. Mercy Macjones, thank you for your love, support, and your sacrifice for me and the family; for being my helpmate in the Gospel and leading the work in Africa – thank you. To my children, David, Grace, Isaac Favour, and Sarah, thank you for your support, love, and understanding, when daddy was away writing and working; and throughout the tough times we have been through together.

To all God Pleasers Family Church and leaders for standing with me and pushing me on throughout all the tough times – I say thank you.

INTRODUCTION

We are facing a very critical time in our nation and around the world. The United States of America has been blessed by God and the world has benefited greatly. There are tough times everywhere and people are panicking. Fear is taking hold of people and men's hearts are fainting and failing them. However, in the midst of this, the Lord is saying to you that tough times never last, so never give up!

The good news is this, God never changes; what He did before, He will do again, He will do it now. The same God that helped the children of Israel out of their own tough times, that same God is here today, to bring you out of your tough times. He is faithful, He is merciful, and He is mighty. He never fails!

The secrets you will learn in this book will change your life forever. These keys and secrets have changed millions of people around the world and they will change you, if only you will believe these secrets, receive, and practice them daily, you will see a difference in your life today. Open your spirit and heart as the Spirit of God takes you on this great journey. John 8:29

Stay blessed.

Chapter 1

WHAT ARE TOUGH TIMES?

Tough Times can be defined simply as a recession, famine, drought or bad times. It is a rough time with all kinds of shortages and sufferings; a time of lack and depression. It is a time of severe hardship and terrible hunger.

The Bible warns us that in the last days, there will be tough times; it will be so tough that people will have no hope or rest. There will be no place to hide and only those who will run to Jesus Christ will be secured. Tough times mean difficult times, harsh and hard times, times of despair, trials and turmoil. II Timothy 3:1-4

To make it simple for all my reader to grasp and understand, I will use and acronym.

T- Trials, Temptation, Terrors, and Terrorists

O- Opposition and Obstacles

U- Unusual Struggles and Under Fire

G – Giants and Groaning's

H- Hell and High Water

T- Trouble and Tragedies

I- Impossibilities and Injustice

M- Mountains Everywhere

E- Enemies Everywhere

S- Sorrows and Sufferings

Can you see that? Do you understand how terrible this is? This is the motivation behind this tool in your hands today. The current national and global situations provoked me to write this book in order to help people see clearly what is going on and to offer a solution. The secrets in this book will help you. If you are facing one or more of the situations listed above, then this book is for you. This material is the solution for all your tough times; study and obey the secrets and be blessed.

Let us read Genesis 41, where we are introduced to an era of tough times that is about to happen:

1 And it came to pass at the end of two full years, that
Pharaoh dreamed: and, behold, he stood by the river.[2]
And, behold, there came up out of the river seven well
favored kine and fat fleshed; and they fed in a meadow.[3]
And, behold, seven other kine came up after them out of
the river, ill favored and lean fleshed; and stood by the
other kine upon the brink of the river.

[4] And the ill favored and leanfleshed kine did eat up
the seven well favored and fat kine. So Pharaoh awoke.[5]
And he slept and dreamed the second time: and, behold,
seven ears of corn came up upon one stalk, rank and
good.[6] And, behold, seven thin ears and blasted with
the east wind sprung up after them.[7] And the seven thin
ears devoured the seven rank and full ears. And Pharaoh
awoke, and, behold, it was a dream.

[8] And it came to pass in the morning that his spirit was
troubled; and he sent and called for all the magicians of
Egypt, and all the wise men thereof: and Pharaoh told
them his dream; but there was none that could interpret
them unto Pharaoh.[9] Then spake the chief butler unto
Pharaoh, saying, I do remember my faults this day:[10]
Pharaoh was wroth with his servants, and put me in

ward in the captain of the guard's house, both me and the chief baker:

[11] And we dreamed a dream in one night, I and he; we dreamed each man according to the interpretation of his dream.[12] And there was there with us a young man, an Hebrew, servant to the captain of the guard; and we told him, and he interpreted to us our dreams; to each man according to his dream he did interpret.

[13] And it came to pass, as he interpreted to us, so it was; me he restored unto mine office, and him he hanged.[14] Then Pharaoh sent and called Joseph, and they brought him hastily out of the dungeon: and he shaved himself, and changed his raiment, and came in unto Pharaoh.

[15] And Pharaoh said unto Joseph, I have dreamed a dream, and there is none that can interpret it: and I have heard say of thee, that thou canst understand a dream to interpret it.

[16] And Joseph answered Pharaoh, saying, It is not in me: God shall give Pharaoh an answer of peace.[17] And Pharaoh said unto Joseph, In my dream, behold, I stood upon the bank of the river:[18] And, behold, there came up out of the river seven kine, fatfleshed and well favoured;

and they fed in a meadow: [19] And, behold, seven other
kine came up after them, poor and very ill favoured and
leanfleshed, such as I never saw in all the land of Egypt
for badness:

[20] And the lean and the ill favored kine did eat up the
first seven fat kine: [21] And when they had eaten them
up, it could not be known that they had eaten them; but
they were still ill favored, as at the beginning. So I awoke.
[22] And I saw in my dream, and, behold, seven ears came
up in one stalk, full and good:

[23] And, behold, seven ears, withered, thin, and
blasted with the east wind, sprung up after them:[24] And
the thin ears devoured the seven good ears: and I told
this unto the magicians; but there was none that could
declare it to me.

[25] And Joseph said unto Pharaoh, The dream of
Pharaoh is one: God hath shewed Pharaoh what he is
about to do.[26] The seven good kine are seven years; and
the seven good ears are seven years: the dream is one.

[27] And the seven thin and ill favored kine that came
up after them are seven years; and the seven empty ears
blasted with the east wind shall be seven years of famine.

28 This is the thing which I have spoken unto Pharaoh:
What God is about to do he sheweth unto Pharaoh.

29 Behold, there come seven years of great plenty
throughout all the land of Egypt:

30 And there shall arise after them seven years of
famine; and all the plenty shall be forgotten in the land
of Egypt; and the famine shall consume the land;

31 And the plenty shall not be known in the land by
reason of that famine following; for it shall be very
grievous.

32 And for that the dream was doubled unto Pharaoh
twice; it is because the thing is established by God, and
God will shortly bring it to pass.

33 Now therefore let Pharaoh look out a man discreet
and wise, and set him over the land of Egypt.

34 Let Pharaoh do this, and let him appoint officers
over the land, and take up the fifth part of the land of
Egypt in the seven plenteous years.

35 And let them gather all the food of those good years
that come, and lay up corn under the hand of Pharaoh,
and let them keep food in the cities.

36 And that food shall be for store to the land against the seven years of famine, which shall be in the land of Egypt; that the land perish not through the famine.

37 And the thing was good in the eyes of Pharaoh, and in the eyes of all his servants.

38 And Pharaoh said unto his servants, Can we find such a one as this is, a man in whom the Spirit of God is?

39 And Pharaoh said unto Joseph, Forasmuch as God hath shewed thee all this, there is none so discreet and wise as thou art:

40 Thou shalt be over my house, and according unto thy word shall all my people be ruled: only in the throne will I be greater than thou.

41 And Pharaoh said unto Joseph, See, I have set thee over all the land of Egypt.

42 And Pharaoh took off his ring from his hand, and put it upon Joseph's hand, and arrayed him in vestures of fine linen, and put a gold chain about his neck;

43 And he made him to ride in the second chariot which he had; and they cried before him, Bow the knee: and he made him ruler over all the land of Egypt.

44 And Pharaoh said unto Joseph, I am Pharaoh, and without thee shall no man lift up his hand or foot in all the land of Egypt.

45 And Pharaoh called Joseph's name Zaphnathpaaneah; and he gave him to wife Asenath the daughter of Potipherah priest of On. And Joseph went out over all the land of Egypt.

46 And Joseph was thirty years old when he stood before Pharaoh king of Egypt. And Joseph went out from the presence of Pharaoh, and went throughout all the land of Egypt.

47 And in the seven plenteous years the earth brought forth by handfuls.

48 And he gathered up all the food of the seven years, which were in the land of Egypt, and laid up the food in the cities: the food of the field, which was round about every city, laid he up in the same.

49 And Joseph gathered corn as the sand of the sea, very much, until he left numbering; for it was without number.

50 And unto Joseph were born two sons before the years of famine came, which Asenath the daughter of Potipherah priest of On bare unto him.

**51 And Joseph called the name of the firstborn
Manasseh: For God, said he, hath made me forget all
my toil, and all my father's house.**

**52 And the name of the second called he Ephraim:
For God hath caused me to be fruitful in the land of my
affliction.**

**53 And the seven years of plenteousness, that was in
the land of Egypt, were ended.**

**54 And the seven years of dearth began to come,
according as Joseph had said: and the dearth was in all
lands; but in all the land of Egypt there was bread.**

**55 And when all the land of Egypt was famished, the
people cried to Pharaoh for bread: and Pharaoh said
unto all the Egyptians, Go unto Joseph; what he saith
to you, do. 56 And the famine was over all the face of
the earth: and Joseph opened all the storehouses, and
sold unto the Egyptians; and the famine waxed sore in
the land of Egypt. 57 And all countries came into Egypt to
Joseph for to buy corn; because that the famine was so
sore in all lands.**

Tough times are times when human wisdom fails and everything that man has built collapses. It is a time of economic confusion and chaos. Banks are failing; companies are closing up and facing bankruptcy. Foreclosures are everywhere; people are vacating their homes due to lack of payments, and companies are downsizing and firing people. It is a time of uncertainty with no help anywhere because there is no money to sustain the family. There is unfaithfulness in marriages and various kinds of sickness and diseases are overtaking people everywhere. Bloodshed, terrorisms spreading around the world day by day.

Tough times are times when everything you trusted in has failed – your best friends, the best doctor, the best banks, the best corporations, and the best of everything fails and collapses. It is time of tragedy and hopelessness. This is exactly what was happening in Egypt. As you can see from the passage you just read, things were really terrible in Egypt. It went from bad to worse; the people suffered and cried out and God in His mercies heard their cry by raising up a deliverer and a savior. He raised someone to face the situation and to bring a solution to the people and the entire nation.

God raised up Joseph in the midst of their tough times, a man whom God filled with secrets of what to do to get out of that season of dryness. Tough times are seasons of dryness; times of testing of your faith and faithfulness, and a time to know what you really believe.

Tough times are bitter times when all hell breaks loose on people, rendering them helpless and hopeless with no help.

Tough times can be in different categories and phases:

- Financial Tough Times
- Physical Tough Times
- Marital Tough Times
- Educational Tough Times
- Political Tough Times
- Spiritual Tough Times
- Generational Tough Times
- General Tough Times – i.e. wars, tornadoes, storms, earthquakes, and disasters.

We will look into each of these tough times categories to see how they affect people and families, especially children. There are nations going through tough times right now with no food, water, shelter, peace, joy, electricity, security and schools. The leadership in these nations is so corrupt and full of selfishness and greed that they do not even care about what is happening to the masses. Except God intervenes, these people will continue to suffer tough times and pain. Every tough time usually begins with bad leadership and a lack of understanding. As we will discuss in the next chapters, God is not the author of tough times and hardship. It is bad people and leadership that open the door to problems, pain, and poverty. You will no longer be a victim in the name of Jesus Christ. There is a way out for you.

1 Corinthians 10:13 reads,

> **There hath no temptation taken you but such as is common to man: but God is faithful, who will not suffer you to be tempted above that ye are able; but will with the temptation also make a way to escape, that ye may be able to bear it.**

FINANCIAL TOUGH TIMES

Financial tough times are times of financial hardship. There is no money to buy, spend or invest; every investment is ruined and unproductive and there are no contracts or income of any kind coming in. In tough times, there is not enough currency in circulation. This is just the situation we are currently witnessing today in our great nation, America, where only a few have access to money to spend.

When banks are facing bankruptcy, what will individuals do? The Lord God, Jehovah Jireh will simply provide.

PHYSICAL TOUGH TIMES

Physical tough times are times when it seems as if all hell has broken loose on you, especially in your health. There are all kinds of diseases and sickness overtaking people today. I am talking about incurable diseases that doctors are saying they do not have a cure for. The list is so long that we will mention just a few, but the Lord God is in control and will heal you today.

- HIV
- Diabetes
- Cancer
- Leukemia
- Ebola
- Zika virius
- High Blood Pressure
- Leprosy

- Epilepsy

Since this is not a book to advertise Satan, we will stop here. There are many dangerous diseases, but Jesus is still the healer and He will heal you today.

MARITAL TOUGH TIMES

Marital tough times are times of family crisis and abandonment, a time of unfaithfulness to your spouse and rejection of responsibility. Divorce is on the rise today like never before. Parents are abandoning their responsibilities and running away. We have a society where single mothers are raising the kids by themselves. What kind of a future are we creating? It is a future where children are raising themselves with both parents not around, a future without parents, no father, and no mentors.

Everything God designed concerning the family has been destroyed by homosexuals, transgenders and unfaithful parents who will not obey God. The issue of divorce is so bad that the government does not know exactly what to do. However, God has the solution and it is here and now. Study it, embrace it and your tough times will be over in Jesus' name. Expect change!

EDUCATIONAL TOUGH TIMES

There are too many schools today with only few students in them. The rate of school dropouts is on the increase due to tough times. Only a few can afford the tuition or fees. Many have dropped out because they could not afford the payments or are no longer interested in school because of bad lifestyles and bad choices. With no sound counsel about education, the gang members in schools are a threat to students. I am sure you must have heard, seen or read about all the recent killings in our schools. These are tough times.

POLITICAL TOUGH TIMES

Political tough times are times when our elected officials, who promised us heaven on earth, begin to back out of their promises. For example, the New York case, the Chicago issue, and the entire political mess going on right now. Only God will save His people from the political tough times going on. That is why this book is a tool to address and arrest the situation of tough times, to show you what to do to overcome the tough times. You must not give up because there is a way out. New leaders are emerging that will lead this nation forward into the promises of God. Don't give up!

SPIRITUAL TOUGH TIMES

Spiritual tough times are times when people lose their spiritual bearings, forget their roots and turn their backs on the spiritual laws and principles that made them great. People today do not even know if there is a God or not. They no longer know what they believe in. When people lose their spiritual connection, they are in trouble. The Bible says in Romans 8, ***"as many as are led by the Spirit of God, they are the sons of God"*** and in Romans 8:14-17, [14] ***For as many as are led by the Spirit of God, they are the sons of God.*** [15] ***For ye have not received the spirit of bondage again to fear; but ye have received the Spirit of adoption, whereby we cry, Abba, Father.*** [16] ***The Spirit itself beareth witness with our spirit, that we are the children of God:***

[17] ***And if children, then heirs; heirs of God, and joint-heirs with Christ; if so be that we suffer with him, that we may be also glorified together.***

Until we allow the Spirit of God to guide, lead, and teach us, we will struggle spiritually and suffer tough times. That is why 1 Corinthians 2:9-14 is the answer for spiritual tough times (1 Corinthians 2:9-14).

[9] But as it is written, Eye hath not seen, nor ear heard, neither have entered into the heart of man, the things which God hath prepared for them that love him.[10] But God hath revealed them unto us by his Spirit: for the Spirit searcheth all things, yea, the deep things of God.[11] For what man knoweth the things of a man, save the spirit of man which is in him? even so the things of God knoweth no man, but the Spirit of God.[12] Now we have received, not the spirit of the world, but the spirit which is of God; that we might know the things that are freely given to us of God.[13] Which things also we speak, not in the words which man's wisdom teacheth, but which the Holy Ghost teacheth; comparing spiritual things with spiritual.[14] But the natural man receiveth not the things of the Spirit of God: for they are foolishness unto him: neither can he know them, because they are spiritually discerned.

GENERAL TOUGH TIMES

General tough times cover issues like wars, tornadoes, cyclones, earthquakes, storms, and disasters. Terrorism, racial battles, blood sheads

The Bible warns us of these evil days and times, but God gave us the solution – His Word and His Spirit. Let us read Matthew 24.

1And Jesus went out, and departed from the temple: and his disciples came to him for to shew him the buildings of the temple. [2] And Jesus said unto them, See ye not all these things? verily I say unto you, There shall not be left here one stone upon another, that shall not be thrown down

.[3] And as he sat upon the mount of Olives, the disciples came unto him privately, saying, Tell us, when shall these things be? and what shall be the sign of thy coming, and of the end of the world?[4] And Jesus answered and said unto them, Take heed that no man deceive you.[5] For many shall come in my name, saying, I am Christ; and shall deceive many.

[6] And ye shall hear of wars and rumors of wars: see that ye be not troubled: for all these things must come to pass, but the end is not yet.[7] For nation shall rise against

nation, and kingdom against kingdom: and there shall
be famines, and pestilences, and earthquakes, in divers
places.[8] All these are the beginning of sorrows.
[9] Then shall they deliver you up to be afflicted, and
shall kill you: and ye shall be hated of all nations for my
name's sake.[10] And then shall many be offended, and
shall betray one another, and shall hate one another.[11]
And many false prophets shall rise, and shall deceive
many.[12] And because iniquity shall abound, the love of
many shall wax cold.[13] But he that shall endure unto the
end, the same shall be saved.[14] And this gospel of the
kingdom shall be preached in all the world for a witness
unto all nations; and then shall the end come.
[15] When ye therefore shall see the abomination of
desolation, spoken of by Daniel the prophet, stand in the
holy place, (whoso readeth, let him understand:) [16] Then
let them which be in Judaea flee into the mountains: [17]
Let him which is on the housetop not come down to take
anything out of his house:
[18] Neither let him which is in the field return back
to take his clothes.[19] And woe unto them that are with
child, and to them that give suck in those days [20] But pray
ye that your flight be not in the winter, neither on the

sabbath day: 21 For then shall be great tribulation, such as was not since the beginning of the world to this time, no, nor ever shall be.

22 And except those days should be shortened, there should no flesh be saved: but for the elect's sake those days shall be shortened. 23 Then if any man shall say unto you, Lo, here is Christ, or there; believe it not. 24 For there shall arise false Christs, and false prophets, and shall shew great signs and wonders; insomuch that, if it were possible, they shall deceive the very elect.

25 Behold, I have told you before. 26 Wherefore if they shall say unto you, Behold, he is in the desert; go not forth: behold, he is in the secret chambers; believe it not. 27 For as the lightning cometh out of the east, and shineth even unto the west; so shall also the coming of the Son of man be. 28 For where so ever the carcass is, there will the eagles be gathered together.

29 Immediately after the tribulation of those days shall the sun be darkened, and the moon shall not give her light, and the stars shall fall from heaven, and the powers of the heavens shall be shaken:

30 And then shall appear the sign of the Son of man in heaven: and then shall all the tribes of the earth mourn,

and they shall see the Son of man coming in the clouds of heaven with power and great glory.

***[31] And he shall send his angels with a great sound of a trumpet, and they shall gather together his elect from
the four winds, from one end of heaven to the other.[32]
Now learn a parable of the fig tree; When his branch is yet tender, and putteth forth leaves, ye know that
summer is nigh: [33] So likewise ye, when ye shall see all
these things, know that it is near, even at the doors.[34]
Verily I say unto you, This generation shall not pass, till
all these things be fulfilled.[35] Heaven and earth shall pass
away, but my words shall not pass away.[36] But of that day and hour knoweth no man, no, not the angels of
heaven, but my Father only.[37] But as the days of Noah
were, so shall also the coming of the Son of man be.[38]
For as in the days that were before the flood they were eating and drinking, marrying and giving in marriage, until the day that Noe entered into the ark,***

***[39] And knew not until the flood came, and took them all away; so shall also the coming of the Son of man
be.[40] Then shall two be in the field; the one shall be
taken, and the other left.[41] Two women shall be grinding
at the mill; the one shall be taken, and the other left.[42]***

Watch therefore: for ye know not what hour your Lord doth come.[43] But know this, that if the good man of the house had known in what watch the thief would come, he would have watched, and would not have suffered his house to be broken up.

[44] Therefore be ye also ready: for in such an hour as ye think not the Son of man cometh.[45] Who then is a faithful and wise servant, whom his lord hath made ruler over his household, to give them meat in due season?[46] Blessed is that servant, whom his lord when he cometh shall find so doing.[47] Verily I say unto you, that he shall make him ruler over all his goods.[48] But and if that evil servant shall say in his heart, My lord delayeth his coming;[49] And shall begin to smite his fellow servants, and to eat and drink with the drunken; [50] The lord of that servant shall come in a day when he looketh not for him, and in an hour that he is not aware of,

[51] And shall cut him asunder, and appoint him his portion with the hypocrites: there shall be weeping and gnashing of teeth.

Chapter 2

WHY THE TOUGH TIMES?

The Bible is clear as to why we go through tough times. The book of John chapter 10 verse 10 states "***the thief cometh not, but for to steal, and to kill, and to destroy: I am come that they might have life, and that they might have it more abundantly.***" Satan is behind every tough time.

We are going to be looking at five major reasons for tough times, although there are more than five. However, we are focusing on only five that really matter:

WHY TOUGH TIMES?

1) Lack of Knowledge Hosea 4:6
2) Bad Choices Deuteronomy 30:19

3) Satanic Attacks Ephesians 6:12
4) DisobedienceIsaiah 1:19-20
5) General Persecution Matthew 13; John 16:33

As long as you live on this planet earth, you will go through tough times, overcome your tough times, and live victoriously. It is God's will for you to live the blessed life.

We are going to be looking at the five major reasons for tough times and see where you are, and what you can correct in your life to move yourself out of your time times. Remember tough times never last!

REASON 1
LACK OF KNOWLEGDE

Hosea 4:6 states, "My people are destroyed for lack of knowledge: because thou hast rejected knowledge, I will also reject thee, that thou shalt be no priest to me: seeing thou hast forgotten the law of thy God, I will also forget thy children."

The Bible says for lack of knowledge the people perish. Which people? God's people, of course. When you do not have knowledge about your victory in Christ Jesus, the enemy will take you through tough times. So as a believer, the first thing is to go for knowledge; knowing exactly who you are.

There are five areas of knowledge you must acquire in order for you to be strong and victorious in life. They are:

- The knowledge of God
- The knowledge of Jesus
- The knowledge of the Holy Spirit
- The knowledge of who you are
- The knowledge of your enemy

To neglect this knowledge is to harm yourself. You must know that tough times never last. Go for knowledge.

REASON 2
BAD CHOICES

In Deuteronomy 30:19 God is very clear about our power of choice: ***"I call heaven and earth to record this day against you, that I have set before you life and death, blessing and cursing: therefore choose life, that both thou and thy seed may live I call heaven and earth to record this day"***

People go through tough times in life because of bad choices. Nobody lives life by chance but by choice. God has given us the power of choice. You are to choose how your destiny turns out. Nobody will make that choice for you. You have been given the power and responsibility to make choices that will bless you and change you.

Joshua 24:14-15 reads,

14 Now therefore fear the LORD, and serve him in sincerity and in truth: and put away the gods which your fathers served on the other side of the flood, and in Egypt; and serve ye the LORD.

15 And if it seem evil unto you to serve the LORD, choose you this day whom ye will serve; whether the gods which your fathers served that were on the other side of the flood, or the gods of the Amorites, in whose land ye dwell: but as for me and my house, we will serve the LORD.

People are making wrong choices daily and those choices take them far away from God and their destiny. They go through unending struggles due to the choices they have made in life. However, in the name of Jesus there is hope for you. Change your choices and change your life today. The story of Israel is a great example of people making bad choices.

Deuteronomy 8 reads,

1 All the commandments which I command thee this day shall ye observe to do, that ye may live, and multiply, and go in and possess the land which the LORD sware unto your fathers.[2] And thou shalt remember all the way which the LORD thy God led thee these forty years in the wilderness, to humble thee, and to prove thee, to know what was in thine heart, whether thou wouldest keep his commandments, or no.[3] And he humbled thee, and suffered thee to hunger, and fed thee with manna, which thou knewest not, neither did thy fathers know; that he might make thee know that man doth not live by bread only, but by every word that proceedeth out of the mouth of the LORD doth man live.

[4] Thy raiment waxed not old upon thee, neither did thy foot swell, these forty years.[5] Thou shalt also consider in thine heart, that, as a man chasteneth his son, so the LORD thy God chasteneth thee.

[6] Therefore thou shalt keep the commandments of the LORD thy God, to walk in his ways, and to fear him.[7] For

***the LORD thy God bringeth thee into a good land, a land
of brooks of water, of fountains and depths that spring
out of valleys and hills; [8] A land of wheat, and barley,
and vines, and fig trees, and pomegranates; a land of oil
olive, and honey; [9] A land wherein thou shalt eat bread
without scarceness, thou shalt not lack any thing in it; a
land whose stones are iron, and out of whose hills thou
mayest dig brass.***

***[10] When thou hast eaten and art full, then thou shalt
bless the LORD thy God for the good land which he hath
given thee.[11] Beware that thou forget not the LORD thy
God, in not keeping his commandments, and his judg-
ments, and his statutes, which I command thee this day:***

***[12] Lest when thou hast eaten and art full, and hast
built goodly houses, and dwelt therein;[13] And when thy
herds and thy flocks multiply, and thy silver and thy gold
is multiplied, and all that thou hast is multiplied; [14] Then
thine heart be lifted up, and thou forget the LORD thy God,
which brought thee forth out of the land of Egypt, from
the house of bondage;[15] Who led thee through that great
and terrible wilderness, wherein were fiery serpents, and
scorpions, and drought, where there was no water; who
brought thee forth water out of the rock of flint;[16] Who***

fed thee in the wilderness with manna, which thy fathers knew not, that he might humble thee, and that he might prove thee, to do thee good at thy latter end;[17] And thou say in thine heart, My power and the might of mine hand hath gotten me this wealth.

[18] But thou shalt remember the LORD thy God: for it is he that giveth thee power to get wealth, that he may establish his covenant which he sware unto thy fathers, as it is this day.[19] And it shall be, if thou do at all forget the LORD thy God, and walk after other gods, and serve them, and worship them, I testify against you this day that ye shall surely perish.[20] As the nations which the LORD destroyeth before your face, so shall ye perish; because ye would not be obedient unto the voice of the LORD your God.

Let us learn from their mistakes of making bad choices and make good choices today. With good choices, you will overcome your tough times. Choose to obey God, Jesus, and the Holy Spirit.

REASON 3

SATANIC ATTACKS

Ephesians 6:12-13 reads,

[12] For we wrestle not against flesh and blood, but against principalities, against powers, against the rulers of the darkness of this world, against spiritual wickedness in high places.[13] Wherefore take unto you the whole armor of God, that ye may be able to withstand in the evil day, and having done all, to stand.

People go through tough times, mainly due to demonic or satanic attacks. We live in a fallen world, with all kinds of evil. Satan works through evil people, leaders, and groups to bring about tough times on the innocent ones in the society. However, with the help of God, you will overcome all tough times. The Bible says in 1 Peter 5:8-9, we have a real enemy with real hatred (1 Peter 5:8-9).

[8] Be sober, be vigilant; because your adversary the devil, as a roaring lion, walketh about, seeking whom he may devour:[9] Whom resist stedfast in the faith, knowing that the same afflictions are accomplished in your brethren that are in the world.

Let us look at two major examples from the Bible of people who went through tough times because of satanic attacks.

1. JOB

Job 1 reads,

1 There was a man in the land of Uz, whose name was Job; and that man was perfect and upright, and one that feared God, and eschewed evil. 2 And there were born unto him seven sons and three daughters. 3 His substance also was seven thousand sheep, and three thousand camels, and five hundred yoke of oxen, and five hundred she asses, and a very great household; so that this man was the greatest of all the men of the east. 4 And his sons went and feasted in their houses, everyone his day; and sent and called for their three sisters to eat and to drink with them.

5 And it was so, when the days of their feasting were gone about, that Job sent and sanctified them, and rose up early in the morning, and offered burnt offerings according to the number of them all: for Job said,

It may be that my sons have sinned, and cursed God in their hearts. Thus did Job continually.

[6] Now there was a day when the sons of God came to present themselves before the LORD, and Satan came also among them.

[7] And the LORD said unto Satan, Whence comest thou? Then Satan answered the LORD, and said, From going to and fro in the earth, and from walking up and down in it.[8] And the LORD said unto Satan, Hast thou considered my servant Job, that there is none like him in the earth, a perfect and an upright man, one that feareth God, and escheweth evil?[9] Then Satan answered the LORD, and said, Doth Job fear God for nought?[10] Hast not thou made an hedge about him, and about his house, and about all that he hath on every side? thou hast blessed the work of his hands, and his substance is increased in the land.

[11] But put forth thine hand now, and touch all that he hath, and he will curse thee to thy face. [12] And the LORD said unto Satan, Behold, all that he hath is in thy power; only upon himself put not forth thine hand. So Satan went forth from the presence of the LORD.

***[13] And there was a day when his sons and his daugh-
ters were eating and drinking wine in their eldest brother's house: [14] And there came a messenger unto Job, and
said, The oxen were plowing, and the asses feeding
beside them:[15] And the Sabeans fell upon them, and
took them away; yea, they have slain the servants with
the edge of the sword; and I only am escaped alone to
tell thee.***

[16] While he was yet speaking, there came also another, and said, The fire of God is fallen from heaven, and hath burned up the sheep, and the servants, and consumed them; and I only am escaped alone to tell thee.

***[17] While he was yet speaking, there came also another,
and said, The Chaldeans made out three bands, and
fell upon the camels, and have carried them away, yea,
and slain the servants with the edge of the sword; and
I only am escaped alone to tell thee. [18] While he was
yet speaking, there came also another, and said, Thy
sons and thy daughters were eating and drinking wine in
their eldest brother's house: [19] And, behold, there came a
great wind from the wilderness, and smote the four corners of the house, and it fell upon the young men, and
they are dead; and I only am escaped alone to tell thee.***

[20] Then Job arose, and rent his mantle, and shaved his head, and fell down upon the ground, and worshipped,[21] And said, Naked came I out of my mother's womb, and naked shall I return thither: the LORD gave, and the LORD hath taken away; blessed be the name of the LORD.[22] In all this Job sinned not, nor charged God foolishly.

2. JESUS

Luke 4:1-14

1 And Jesus being full of the Holy Ghost returned from Jordan, and was led by the Spirit into the wilderness,[2] Being forty days tempted of the devil. And in those days he did eat nothing: and when they were ended, he afterward hungered.[3] And the devil said unto him, If thou be the Son of God, command this stone that it be made bread.[4] And Jesus answered him, saying, It is written, That man shall not live by bread alone, but by every word of God.[5] And the devil, taking him up into an high mountain, shewed unto him all the kingdoms of the world in a moment of time.[6] And the devil said unto him, All this power will I give thee, and the glory of them: for that is delivered unto me; and to whomsoever

I will I give it. [7] If thou therefore wilt worship me, all shall be thine.

[8] And Jesus answered and said unto him, Get thee behind me, Satan: for it is written, Thou shalt worship the Lord thy God, and him only shalt thou serve.[9] And he brought him to Jerusalem, and set him on a pinnacle of the temple, and said unto him, If thou be the Son of God, cast thyself down from hence: [10] For it is written, He shall give his angels charge over thee, to keep thee: [11] And in their hands they shall bear thee up, lest at any time thou dash thy foot against a stone.[12] And Jesus answering said unto him, It is said, Thou shalt not tempt the Lord thy God.[13] And when the devil had ended all the temptation, he departed from him for a season.[14] And Jesus returned in the power of the Spirit into Galilee: and there went out a fame of him through all the region round about.

From these stories you can see that Satan was behind every temptation, trial, and attack. However, in the midst of it all they overcame. Therefore, so shall you overcome your tough times in Jesus' name. God is bringing you out now in Jesus' name.

Philippians 2:8-10 reads,

[8] And being found in fashion as a man, he humbled himself, and became obedient unto death, even the death of the cross.[9] Wherefore God also hath highly exalted him, and given him a name which is above every name:[10] That at the name of Jesus every knee should bow, of things in heaven, and things in earth, and things under the earth;

REASON 4
DISOBEDIENCE

Isaiah 1:19-20 reads,

[19] If ye be willing and obedient, ye shall eat the good of the land:[20] But if ye refuse and rebel, ye shall be devoured with the sword: for the mouth of the LORD hath spoken it.

Job 36:11-12 reads,

[11] If they obey and serve him, they shall spend their days in prosperity, and their years in pleasures.[12] But if they obey not, they shall perish by the sword, and they shall die without knowledge.

The Bible says obedience is better than sacrifice. People go through tough times because of disobedience. They disobey God, His plans for them, His will for them, and His purpose for them. When you are operating in disobedience, life will be tough. Nobody disobeys God and wins in life. When you walk in disobedience, tough times await you.

When you study the majority of people, families or nations that are experiencing tough times, it can be related to disobedience. The Bible is covered with such stories. Let us look at two such examples of disobedience in the persons of King Saul and Jonah.

1. King Saul
1 Samuel 15:1-35

1 Samuel also said unto Saul, The LORD sent me to anoint thee to be king over his people, over Israel: now therefore hearken thou unto the voice of the words of the LORD.2 Thus saith the LORD of hosts, I remember that which Amalek did to Israel, how he laid wait for him in the way, when he came up from Egypt.3 Now go and smite Amalek, and utterly destroy all that they have, and spare them not; but slay both man and woman, infant

and suckling, ox and sheep, camel and ass.[4] And Saul
gathered the people together, and numbered them in
Telaim, two hundred thousand footmen, and ten thou-
sand men of Judah.[5] And Saul came to a city of Amalek,
and laid wait in the valley.[6] And Saul said unto the Kenites,
Go, depart, get you down from among the Amalekites,
lest I destroy you with them: for ye shewed kindness to
all the children of Israel, when they came up out of Egypt.
So the Kenites departed from among the Amalekites.[7]
And Saul smote the Amalekites from Havilah until thou
comest to Shur, that is over against Egypt.

[8] And he took Agag the king of the Amalekites alive,
and utterly destroyed all the people with the edge of
the sword.[9] But Saul and the people spared Agag, and
the best of the sheep, and of the oxen, and of the fat-
lings, and the lambs, and all that was good, and would
not utterly destroy them: but everything that was vile
and refuse, that they destroyed utterly.[10] Then came the
word of the LORD unto Samuel, saying,[11] It repenteth me
that I have set up Saul to be king: for he is turned back
from following me, and hath not performed my com-
mandments. And it grieved Samuel; and he cried unto
the LORD all night.

[12] And when Samuel rose early to meet Saul in the morning, it was told Samuel, saying, Saul came to Carmel, and, behold, he set him up a place, and is gone about, and passed on, and gone down to Gilgal.[13] And Samuel came to Saul: and Saul said unto him, Blessed be thou of the LORD: I have performed the commandment of the LORD.

[14] And Samuel said, What meaneth then this bleating of the sheep in mine ears, and the lowing of the oxen which I hear? [15] And Saul said, They have brought them from the Amalekites: for the people spared the best of the sheep and of the oxen, to sacrifice unto the LORD thy God; and the rest we have utterly destroyed. [16] Then Samuel said unto Saul, Stay, and I will tell thee what the LORD hath said to me this night. And he said unto him, Say on.

[17] And Samuel said, When thou wast little in thine own sight, wast thou not made the head of the tribes of Israel, and the LORD anointed thee king over Israel? [18] And the LORD sent thee on a journey, and said, Go and utterly destroy the sinners the Amalekites, and fight against them until they be consumed. [19] Wherefore then

*didst thou not obey the voice of the LORD, but didst fly
upon the spoil, and didst evil in the sight of the LORD?*

*[20] And Saul said unto Samuel, Yea, I have obeyed the
voice of the LORD, and have gone the way which the LORD
sent me, and have brought Agag the king of Amalek, and
have utterly destroyed the Amalekites.[21] But the people
took of the spoil, sheep and oxen, the chief of the things
which should have been utterly destroyed, to sacrifice
unto the LORD thy God in Gilgal.*

*[22] And Samuel said, Hath the LORD as great delight in
burnt offerings and sacrifices, as in obeying the voice of
the LORD? Behold, to obey is better than sacrifice, and
to hearken than the fat of rams.*

*[23] For rebellion is as the sin of witchcraft, and stub-
bornness is as iniquity and idolatry. Because thou hast
rejected the word of the LORD, he hath also rejected thee
from being king. [24] And Saul said unto Samuel, I have
sinned: for I have transgressed the commandment of the
LORD, and thy words: because I feared the people, and
obeyed their voice.*

*[25] Now therefore, I pray thee, pardon my sin, and turn
again with me, that I may worship the LORD.*

***26** And Samuel said unto Saul, I will not return with thee: for thou hast rejected the word of the LORD, and the LORD hath rejected thee from being king over Israel.*
***27** And as Samuel turned about to go away, he laid hold upon the skirt of his mantle, and it rent.*

***28** And Samuel said unto him, The LORD hath rent the kingdom of Israel from thee this day, and hath given it to a neighbour of thine, that is better than thou.*

***29** And also the Strength of Israel will not lie nor repent: for he is not a man, that he should repent.*

***30** Then he said, I have sinned: yet honour me now, I pray thee, before the elders of my people, and before Israel, and turn again with me, that I may worship the LORD thy God.*

***31** So Samuel turned again after Saul; and Saul worshipped the LORD.*

***32** Then said Samuel, Bring ye hither to me Agag the king of the Amalekites. And Agag came unto him delicately. And Agag said, Surely the bitterness of death is past.*

***33** And Samuel said, As thy sword hath made women childless, so shall thy mother be childless among women.*

And Samuel hewed Agag in pieces before the LORD in Gilgal.

[34] Then Samuel went to Ramah; and Saul went up to his house to Gibeah of Saul.

[35] And Samuel came no more to see Saul until the day of his death: nevertheless Samuel mourned for Saul: and the LORD repented that he had made Saul king over Israel.

2. JONAH

Jonah 1:1-17

1 Now the word of the LORD came unto Jonah the
son of Amittai, saying,[2] Arise, go to Nineveh, that great
city, and cry against it; for their wickedness is come up
before me.[3] But Jonah rose up to flee unto Tarshish from
the presence of the LORD, and went down to Joppa; and
he found a ship going to Tarshish: so he paid the fare
thereof, and went down into it, to go with them unto
Tarshish from the presence of the LORD.[4] But the LORD
sent out a great wind into the sea, and there was a
mighty tempest in the sea, so that the ship was like to
be broken.

*5 Then the mariners were afraid, and cried every man
unto his god, and cast forth the wares that were in the
ship into the sea, to lighten it of them. But Jonah was
gone down into the sides of the ship; and he lay, and
was fast asleep.*

*6 So the shipmaster came to him, and said unto him,
What meanest thou, O sleeper? arise, call upon thy God,
if so be that God will think upon us, that we perish not.*

*7 And they said every one to his fellow, Come, and let
us cast lots, that we may know for whose cause this evil
is upon us. So they cast lots, and the lot fell upon Jonah.*

*8 Then said they unto him, Tell us, we pray thee, for
whose cause this evil is upon us; What is thine occupa-
tion? and whence comest thou? what is thy country? and
of what people art thou?*

*9 And he said unto them, I am an Hebrew; and I fear
the LORD, the God of heaven, which hath made the sea
and the dry land.*

*10 Then were the men exceedingly afraid, and said
unto him. Why hast thou done this? For the men knew
that he fled from the presence of the LORD, because he
had told them.*

11 Then said they unto him, What shall we do unto thee, that the sea may be calm unto us? for the sea wrought, and was tempestuous.

12 And he said unto them, Take me up, and cast me forth into the sea; so shall the sea be calm unto you: for I know that for my sake this great tempest is upon you.

13 Nevertheless the men rowed hard to bring it to the land; but they could not: for the sea wrought, and was tempestuous against them.

14 Wherefore they cried unto the LORD, and said, We beseech thee, O LORD, we beseech thee, let us not perish for this man's life, and lay not upon us innocent blood: for thou, O LORD, hast done as it pleased thee.

15 So they took up Jonah, and cast him forth into the sea: and the sea ceased from her raging.

16 Then the men feared the LORD exceedingly, and offered a sacrifice unto the LORD, and made vows.

17 Now the LORD had prepared a great fish to swallow up Jonah. And Jonah was in the belly of the fish three days and three nights.

You cannot disobey God and win in tough times. Obey God today and your tough times will be over. When Jonah obeyed God, all his tough times came to an end.

Consequently, you will also see victory as you make the choice today to obey God. Stop running!

REASON 5
GENERAL PERSECUTION

John 16:33 reads,

[33] These things I have spoken unto you, that in me ye might have peace. In the world ye shall have tribulation: but be of good cheer; I have overcome the world.

2 Timothy 3:12 reads,

Yea, and all that will live godly in Christ Jesus shall suffer persecution.

Matthew 13:21

Yet hath he not root himself, but endureth for a while: for when tribulation or persecution ariseth because of the word, by and by he is offended

According to the above scriptures, the Bible says if we live a godly life in this world, we will face tough times, but the good news is that they will come and go, and we will overcome them. Jesus came into this world and faced tough times, but He overcame it all.

When He was leaving the earth, He gave His followers, disciples, and all that believe in Him the same power and authority that He operated in while He was physically here on earth. This was so that we can overcome all the tough times we will ever go through.

As a believer in Jesus Christ, no matter the persecution you go through and no matter the tough times, God will always make a way of escape for you. Remember, "tough times never last but tough people do," said Robert H. Schuller.

In John 16:33 Jesus said, "Be of good cheer, I have overcome the world." The system of this world cannot hold you down. There is no power mightier than Jesus' name. Whatever maybe the reason that you are going through tough times now, God is able and has worked out a way of escape for you.

John 16:33 reads,

33 These things I have spoken unto you, that in me ye might have peace. In the world ye shall have tribulation: but be of good cheer; I have overcome the world.

1 Corinthians 10:13 reads,

[13] There hath no temptation taken you but such as is common to man: but God is faithful, who will not suffer you to be tempted above that ye are able; but will with the temptation also make a way to escape, that ye may be able to bear it.

All you need to do is apply the seven secrets and every trouble will be over in the name of Jesus. Remember, tough times never last, you are an overcomer! The story in the book of John 11 should help and encourage you. They went through tough times as a family, but they came out on top. Your Lazarus will come back to life in the name of Jesus!

John 11 reads,

1 Now a certain man was sick, named Lazarus, of Bethany, the town of Mary and her sister Martha.[2] (It was that Mary which anointed the Lord with ointment, and wiped his feet with her hair, whose brother Lazarus was sick.)[3] Therefore his sisters sent unto him, saying, Lord, behold, he whom thou lovest is sick.[4] When Jesus heard that, he said, This sickness is not unto death, but for the glory of God, that the Son of God might be

glorified thereby. 5 Now Jesus loved Martha, and her
sister, and Lazarus.

6 When he had heard therefore that he was sick, he
abode two days still in the same place where he was. 7
Then after that saith he to his disciples, Let us go into
Judaea again. 8 His disciples say unto him, Master, the
Jews of late sought to stone thee; and goest thou thither
again? 9 Jesus answered, Are there not twelve hours in
the day? If any man walk in the day, he stumbleth not,
because he seeth the light of this world. 10 But if a man
walk in the night, he stumbleth, because there is no
light in him.

11 These things said he: and after that he saith unto
them, Our friend Lazarus sleepeth; but I go, that I may
awake him out of sleep. 12 Then said his disciples, Lord, if
he sleep, he shall do well. 13 Howbeit Jesus spake of his
death: but they thought that he had spoken of taking of
rest in sleep. 14 Then said Jesus unto them plainly, Lazarus
is dead. 15 And I am glad for your sakes that I was not there,
to the intent ye may believe; nevertheless let us go unto
him. 16 Then said Thomas, which is called Didymus, unto
his fellow disciples, Let us also go, that we may die with
him. 17 Then when Jesus came, he found that he had lain

in the grave four days already. 18 Now Bethany was nigh unto Jerusalem, about fifteen furlongs off: 19 And many of the Jews came to Martha and Mary, to comfort them concerning their brother.

20 Then Martha, as soon as she heard that Jesus was coming, went and met him: but Mary sat still in the house. 21 Then said Martha unto Jesus, Lord, if thou hadst been here, my brother had not died.

22 But I know, that even now, whatsoever thou wilt ask of God, God will give it thee. 23 Jesus saith unto her, Thy brother shall rise again. 24 Martha saith unto him, I know that he shall rise again in the resurrection at the last day. 25 Jesus said unto her, I am the resurrection, and the life: he that believeth in me, though he were dead, yet shall he live: 26 And whosoever liveth and believeth in me shall never die. Believest thou this? 27 She saith unto him, Yea, Lord: I believe that thou art the Christ, the Son of God, which should come into the world.

28 And when she had so said, she went her way, and called Mary her sister secretly, saying, The Master is come, and calleth for thee. 29 As soon as she heard that, she arose quickly, and came unto him.

*[30] Now Jesus was not yet come into the town, but was
in that place where Martha met him.*

*[31] The Jews then which were with her in the house,
and comforted her, when they saw Mary, that she rose
up hastily and went out, followed her, saying, She goeth
unto the grave to weep there.*

*[32] Then when Mary was come where Jesus was, and
saw him, she fell down at his feet, saying unto him, Lord,
if thou hadst been here, my brother had not died.*

*[33] When Jesus therefore saw her weeping, and the
Jews also weeping which came with her, he groaned in
the spirit, and was troubled.*

*[34] And said, Where have ye laid him? They said unto
him, Lord, come and see.*

[35] Jesus wept.

[36] Then said the Jews, Behold how he loved him!

*[37] And some of them said, Could not this man, which
opened the eyes of the blind, have caused that even this
man should not have died?*

*[38] Jesus therefore again groaning in himself cometh
to the grave. It was a cave, and a stone lay upon it.*

39 Jesus said, Take ye away the stone. Martha, the
sister of him that was dead, saith unto him, Lord, by this
time he stinketh: for he hath been dead four days.

40 Jesus saith unto her, Said I not unto thee, that, if thou
wouldest believe, thou shouldest see the glory of God?

41 Then they took away the stone from the place
where the dead was laid. And Jesus lifted up his eyes,
and said, Father, I thank thee that thou hast heard me.

42 And I knew that thou hearest me always: but
because of the people which stand by I said it, that they
may believe that thou hast sent me.

43 And when he thus had spoken, he cried with a loud
voice, Lazarus, come forth.

44 And he that was dead came forth, bound hand and
foot with grave clothes: and his face was bound about
with a napkin. Jesus saith unto them, Loose him, and
let him go.

45 Then many of the Jews which came to Mary, and
had seen the things which Jesus did, believed on him.

46 But some of them went their ways to the Pharisees,
and told them what things Jesus had done.

[47] Then gathered the chief priests and the Pharisees a council, and said, What do we? for this man doeth many miracles.

[48] If we let him thus alone, all men will believe on him: and the Romans shall come and take away both our place and nation.

[49] And one of them, named Caiaphas, being the high priest that same year, said unto them, Ye know nothing at all,

[50] Nor consider that it is expedient for us, that one man should die for the people, and that the whole nation perish not.

[51] And this spake he not of himself: but being high priest that year, he prophesied that Jesus should die for that nation;

[52] And not for that nation only, but that also he should gather together in one the children of God that were scattered abroad.

[53] Then from that day forth they took counsel together for to put him to death.

[54] Jesus therefore walked no more openly among the Jews; but went thence unto a country near to the

wilderness, into a city called Ephraim, and there con-
tinued with his disciples.

55 And the Jews' passover was nigh at hand: and
many went out of the country up to Jerusalem before
the passover, to purify themselves.

56 Then sought they for Jesus, and spake among them-
selves, as they stood in the temple, What think ye, that
he will not come to the feast?

57 Now both the chief priests and the Pharisees had
given a commandment, that, if any man knew where he
were, he should shew it, that they might take him.

Never give up; you are next in line for a miracle. Remember, tough times never last. If Lazaurus came forth, your miracles and breakthroughs are coming forth in Jesus' name. He is the same yesterday, today, and forever more. Just believe in Him!

Chapter 3

EXAMPLES OF TOUGH TIMES IN THE BIBLE

We want to take a look at the examples of the tough times in the Bible and see what lesson we can learn from them. That will also assure our hearts that if they survived it, we will, too. If they overcame their tough times, we will, too. In Job 5:19-22, we read,

19 He shall deliver thee in six troubles: yea, in seven there shall no evil touch thee. 20 In famine he shall redeem thee from death: and in war from the power of the sword. 21 Thou shalt be hid from the scourge of the tongue: neither shalt thou be afraid of destruction when it cometh. 22 At destruction and famine thou shalt laugh: neither shalt thou be afraid of the beasts of the earth.

ROMANS 8:35

*[35] **Who shall separate us from the love of Christ? shall tribulation, or distress, or persecution, or famine, or nakedness, or peril, or sword?***

Many times in the Old Testament, they referred to tough times as famine in the land or drought.

FAMINE/TOUGH TIMES #1

In Genesis 12 we see Abraham's tough times and how he overcame them.

1 Now the LORD had said unto Abram, Get thee out of thy country, and from thy kindred, and from thy father's house, unto a land that I will shew thee:[2] And I will make of thee a great nation, and I will bless thee, and make thy name great; and thou shalt be a blessing:[3] And I will bless them that bless thee, and curse him that curseth thee: and in thee shall all families of the earth be blessed.

[4] So Abram departed, as the LORD had spoken unto him; and Lot went with him: and Abram was seventy and five years old when he departed out of Haran.

[5] And Abram took Sarai his wife, and Lot his brother's son, and all their substance that they had gathered, and

the souls that they had gotten in Haran; and they went forth to go into the land of Canaan; and into the land of Canaan they came.

6 And Abram passed through the land unto the place of Sichem, unto the plain of Moreh. And the Canaanite was then in the land.

7 And the LORD appeared unto Abram, and said, Unto thy seed will I give this land: and there builded he an altar unto the LORD, who appeared unto him.

8 And he removed from thence unto a mountain on the east of Bethel, and pitched his tent, having Bethel on the west, and Hai on the east: and there he builded an altar unto the LORD, and called upon the name of the LORD.

9 And Abram journeyed, going on still toward the south.

10 And there was a famine in the land: and Abram went down into Egypt to sojourn there; for the famine was grievous in the land.

11 And it came to pass, when he was come near to enter into Egypt, that he said unto Sarai his wife, Behold now, I know that thou art a fair woman to look upon:

[12] Therefore it shall come to pass, when the Egyptians shall see thee, that they shall say, This is his wife: and they will kill me, but they will save thee alive.

[13] Say, I pray thee, thou art my sister: that it may be well with me for thy sake; and my soul shall live because of thee.

[14] And it came to pass, that, when Abram was come into Egypt, the Egyptians beheld the woman that she was very fair.

[15] The princes also of Pharaoh saw her, and commended her before Pharaoh: and the woman was taken into Pharaoh's house.[16] And he entreated Abram well for her sake: and he had sheep, and oxen, and he asses, and menservants, and maidservants, and she asses, and camels.

[17] And the LORD plagued Pharaoh and his house with great plagues because of Sarai Abram's wife.[18] And Pharaoh called Abram and said, What is this that thou hast done unto me? why didst thou not tell me that she was thy wife?

[19] Why saidst thou, She is my sister? so I might have taken her to me to wife: now therefore behold thy wife, take her, and go thy way.[20] And Pharaoh commanded his

men concerning him: and they sent him away, and his wife, and all that he had.

If Abraham overcame his tough times by obeying God, I promise you that you too will overcome yours. Simply apply the secrets and you will experience victory.

FAMINE/TOUGH TIME #2

In Genesis 26, we are told of the tough times during Isaac's time and how he overcame them.

1 And there was a famine in the land, beside the first famine that was in the days of Abraham. And Isaac went unto Abimelech king of the Philistines unto Gerar. 2 ***And the LORD appeared unto him, and said, Go not down into Egypt; dwell in the land which I shall tell thee of:***
3 ***Sojourn in this land, and I will be with thee, and will bless thee; for unto thee, and unto thy seed, I will give all these countries, and I will perform the oath which I sware unto Abraham thy father;***

4 ***And I will make thy seed to multiply as the stars of heaven, and will give unto thy seed all these countries; and in thy seed shall all the nations of the earth be blessed;***

5 Because that Abraham obeyed my voice, and kept my charge, my commandments, my statutes, and my laws.

6 And Isaac dwelt in Gerar:

7 And the men of the place asked him of his wife; and he said, She is my sister: for he feared to say, She is my wife; lest, said he, the men of the place should kill me for Rebekah; because she was fair to look upon.

8 And it came to pass, when he had been there a long time, that Abimelech king of the Philistines looked out at a window, and saw, and, behold, Isaac was sporting with Rebekah his wife.

9 And Abimelech called Isaac, and said, Behold, of a surety she is thy wife; and how saidst thou, She is my sister? And Isaac said unto him, Because I said, Lest I die for her.

10 And Abimelech said, What is this thou hast done unto us? one of the people might lightly have lien with thy wife, and thou shouldest have brought guiltiness upon us.

11 And Abimelech charged all his people, saying, He that toucheth this man or his wife shall surely be put to death.

***12 Then Isaac sowed in that land, and received in the
same year an hundredfold: and the LORD blessed him.***

***13 And the man waxed great, and went forward, and
grew until he became very great:***

***14 For he had possession of flocks, and possession of
herds, and great store of servants: and the Philistines
envied him.***

***15 For all the wells which his father's servants had
digged in the days of Abraham his father, the Philistines
had stopped them, and filled them with earth.***

***16 And Abimelech said unto Isaac, Go from us; for thou
art much mightier than we.***

***17 And Isaac departed thence, and pitched his tent in
the valley of Gerar, and dwelt there.***

***18 And Isaac digged again the wells of water, which
they had digged in the days of Abraham his father; for
the Philistines had stopped them after the death of
Abraham: and he called their names after the names by
which his father had called them.***

***19 And Isaac's servants digged in the valley, and found
there a well of springing water.***

[20] And the herdmen of Gerar did strive with Isaac's herdmen, saying, The water is ours: and he called the name of the well Esek; because they strove with him.

[21] And they digged another well, and strove for that also: and he called the name of it Sitnah.

[22] And he removed from thence, and digged another well; and for that they strove not: and he called the name of it Rehoboth; and he said, For now the LORD hath made room for us, and we shall be fruitful in the land.

[23] And he went up from thence to Beersheba.

[24] And the LORD appeared unto him the same night, and said, I am the God of Abraham thy father: fear not, for I am with thee, and will bless thee, and multiply thy seed for my servant Abraham's sake.

[25] And he builded an altar there, and called upon the name of the LORD, and pitched his tent there: and there Isaac's servants digged a well.

[26] Then Abimelech went to him from Gerar, and Ahuzzath one of his friends, and Phichol the chief captain of his army.

[27] And Isaac said unto them, Wherefore come ye to me, seeing ye hate me, and have sent me away from you?

28 And they said, We saw certainly that the LORD was with thee: and we said, Let there be now an oath betwixt us, even betwixt us and thee, and let us make a covenant with thee;

29 That thou wilt do us no hurt, as we have not touched thee, and as we have done unto thee nothing but good, and have sent thee away in peace: thou art now the blessed of the LORD.

30 And he made them a feast, and they did eat and drink.

31 And they rose up betimes in the morning, and sware one to another: and Isaac sent them away, and they departed from him in peace.

32 And it came to pass the same day, that Isaac's servants came, and told him concerning the well which they had digged, and said unto him, We have found water.

33 And he called it Shebah: therefore the name of the city is Beersheba unto this day.

34 And Esau was forty years old when he took to wife Judith the daughter of Beeri the Hittite, and Bashemath the daughter of Elon the Hittite:

35 Which were a grief of mind unto Isaac and to Rebekah.

If Isaac overcame his tough times, so will you.

FAMINE/TOUGH TIMES #3

Genesis 41:1-57 reveals that the tough times that transpired in Egypt during the era of Joseph was the worst of all the famines in the Bible. These were terrible times.

1 And it came to pass at the end of two full years, that
Pharaoh dreamed: and, behold, he stood by the river.[2]
And, behold, there came up out of the river seven well
favored kine and fatfleshed; and they fed in a meadow.[3]
And, behold, seven other kine came up after them out
of the river, ill-favored and leanfleshed; and stood by
the other kine upon the brink of the river.[4] And the ill-fa-
vored and leanfleshed kine did eat up the seven well
favored and fat kine. So Pharaoh awoke.[5] And he slept
and dreamed the second time: and, behold, seven ears
of corn came up upon one stalk, rank and good.

[6] And, behold, seven thin ears and blasted with the east wind sprung up after them.

[7] And the seven thin ears devoured the seven rank and full ears. And Pharaoh awoke, and, behold, it was a dream.

***8** And it came to pass in the morning that his spirit was troubled; and he sent and called for all the magicians of Egypt, and all the wise men thereof: and Pharaoh told them his dream; but there was none that could interpret them unto Pharaoh.*

***9** Then spake the chief butler unto Pharaoh, saying, I do remember my faults this day:*

***10** Pharaoh was wroth with his servants, and put me in ward in the captain of the guard's house, both me and the chief baker:*

***11** And we dreamed a dream in one night, I and he; we dreamed each man according to the interpretation of his dream.*

***12** And there was there with us a young man, an Hebrew, servant to the captain of the guard; and we told him, and he interpreted to us our dreams; to each man according to his dream he did interpret.*

***13** And it came to pass, as he interpreted to us, so it was; me he restored unto mine office, and him he hanged.*

***14** Then Pharaoh sent and called Joseph, and they brought him hastily out of the dungeon: and he shaved himself, and changed his raiment, and came in unto Pharaoh.*

15 And Pharaoh said unto Joseph, I have dreamed a
dream, and there is none that can interpret it: and I have
heard say of thee, that thou canst understand a dream
to interpret it.

16 And Joseph answered Pharaoh, saying, It is not in
me: God shall give Pharaoh an answer of peace.

17 And Pharaoh said unto Joseph, In my dream, behold,
I stood upon the bank of the river:

18 And, behold, there came up out of the river seven
kine, fatfleshed and well favoured; and they fed in
a meadow:

19 And, behold, seven other kine came up after them,
poor and very ill favoured and leanfleshed, such as I
never saw in all the land of Egypt for badness:

20 And the lean and the ill-favored kine did eat up the
first seven fat kine:

21 And when they had eaten them up, it could not be
known that they had eaten them; but they were still ill
favored, as at the beginning. So I awoke.

22 And I saw in my dream, and, behold, seven ears
came up in one stalk, full and good:

23 And, behold, seven ears, withered, thin, and blasted
with the east wind, sprung up after them:

*24 And the thin ears devoured the seven good ears:
and I told this unto the magicians; but there was none
that could declare it to me.*

*25 And Joseph said unto Pharaoh, The dream of
Pharaoh is one: God hath shewed Pharaoh what he is
about to do.*

*26 The seven good kine are seven years; and the seven
good ears are seven years: the dream is one.*

*27 And the seven thin and ill-favored kine that came
up after them are seven years; and the seven empty ears
blasted with the east wind shall be seven years of famine.*

*28 This is the thing which I have spoken unto Pharaoh:
What God is about to do he sheweth unto Pharaoh.*

*29 Behold, there come seven years of great plenty
throughout all the land of Egypt:*

*30 And there shall arise after them seven years of
famine; and all the plenty shall be forgotten in the land
of Egypt; and the famine shall consume the land;*

*31 And the plenty shall not be known in the land by
reason of that famine following; for it shall be very
grievous.*

*[32] And for that the dream was doubled unto Pharaoh
twice; it is because the thing is established by God, and
God will shortly bring it to pass.*

*[33] Now therefore let Pharaoh look out a man discreet
and wise, and set him over the land of Egypt.*

*[34] Let Pharaoh do this, and let him appoint officers
over the land, and take up the fifth part of the land of
Egypt in the seven plenteous years.*

*[35] And let them gather all the food of those good years
that come, and lay up corn under the hand of Pharaoh,
and let them keep food in the cities.*

*[36] And that food shall be for store to the land against
the seven years of famine, which shall be in the land of
Egypt; that the land perish not through the famine.*

*[37] And the thing was good in the eyes of Pharaoh, and
in the eyes of all his servants.*

*[38] And Pharaoh said unto his servants, Can we find
such a one as this is, a man in whom the Spirit of God is?*

*[39] And Pharaoh said unto Joseph, Forasmuch as God
hath shewed thee all this, there is none so discreet and
wise as thou art:*

40 Thou shalt be over my house, and according unto thy word shall all my people be ruled: only in the throne will I be greater than thou.

41 And Pharaoh said unto Joseph, See, I have set thee over all the land of Egypt.

42 And Pharaoh took off his ring from his hand, and put it upon Joseph's hand, and arrayed him in vestures of fine linen, and put a gold chain about his neck;

43 And he made him to ride in the second chariot which he had; and they cried before him, Bow the knee: and he made him ruler over all the land of Egypt.

44 And Pharaoh said unto Joseph, I am Pharaoh, and without thee shall no man lift up his hand or foot in all the land of Egypt.

45 And Pharaoh called Joseph's name Zaphnathpaaneah; and he gave him to wife Asenath the daughter of Potipherah priest of On. And Joseph went out over all the land of Egypt.

46 And Joseph was thirty years old when he stood before Pharaoh king of Egypt. And Joseph went out from the presence of Pharaoh, and went throughout all the land of Egypt.

*[47] **And in the seven plenteous years the earth brought forth by handfuls.***

*[48] **And he gathered up all the food of the seven years, which were in the land of Egypt, and laid up the food in the cities: the food of the field, which was round about every city, laid he up in the same.***

*[49] **And Joseph gathered corn as the sand of the sea, very much, until he left numbering; for it was without number.***

*[50] **And unto Joseph were born two sons before the years of famine came, which Asenath the daughter of Potipherah priest of On bare unto him.***

*[51] **And Joseph called the name of the firstborn Manasseh: For God, said he, hath made me forget all my toil, and all my father's house.***

*[52] **And the name of the second called he Ephraim: For God hath caused me to be fruitful in the land of my affliction.***

*[53] **And the seven years of plenteousness, that was in the land of Egypt, were ended.***

*[54] **And the seven years of dearth began to come, according as Joseph had said: and the dearth was in all lands; but in all the land of Egypt there was bread.***

[55] And when all the land of Egypt was famished, the people cried to Pharaoh for bread: and Pharaoh said unto all the Egyptians, Go unto Joseph; what he saith to you, do.

[56] And the famine was over all the face of the earth: and Joseph opened all the storehouses, and sold unto the Egyptians; and the famine waxed sore in the land of Egypt.

[57] And all countries came into Egypt to Joseph for to buy corn; because that the famine was so sore in all lands.

Genesis 42:13-31

[13] And they said, Thy servants are twelve brethren, the sons of one man in the land of Canaan; and, behold, the youngest is this day with our father, and one is not.

[14] And Joseph said unto them, That is it that I spake unto you, saying, Ye are spies:

[15] Hereby ye shall be proved: By the life of Pharaoh ye shall not go forth hence, except your youngest brother come hither.

[16] Send one of you, and let him fetch your brother, and ye shall be kept in prison, that your words may be proved, whether there be any truth in you: or else by the life of Pharaoh surely ye are spies.

17 And he put them all together into ward three days.

*18 And Joseph said unto them the third day, This do,
and live; for I fear God:*

*19 If ye be true men, let one of your brethren be bound
in the house of your prison: go ye, carry corn for the
famine of your houses:*

*20 But bring your youngest brother unto me; so
shall your words be verified, and ye shall not die. And
they did so.*

*21 And they said one to another, We are verily guilty
concerning our brother, in that we saw the anguish of
his soul, when he besought us, and we would not hear;
therefore is this distress come upon us.*

*22 And Reuben answered them, saying, Spake I not
unto you, saying, Do not sin against the child; and ye
would not hear? therefore, behold, also his blood is
required.*

*23 And they knew not that Joseph understood them;
for he spake unto them by an interpreter.*

*24 And he turned himself about from them, and wept;
and returned to them again, and communed with them,
and took from them Simeon, and bound him before
their eyes.*

***25 Then Joseph commanded to fill their sacks with
corn, and to restore every man's money into his sack,
and to give them provision for the way: and thus did he
unto them.***

***26 And they laded their asses with the corn, and
departed thence.***

***27 And as one of them opened his sack to give his ass
provender in the inn, he espied his money; for, behold, it
was in his sack's mouth.***

***28 And he said unto his brethren, My money is restored;
and, lo, it is even in my sack: and their heart failed them,
and they were afraid, saying one to another, What is this
that God hath done unto us?***

***29 And they came unto Jacob their father unto the land
of Canaan, and told him all that befell unto them; saying,***

***30 The man, who is the lord of the land, spake roughly
to us, and took us for spies of the country.***

***31 And we said unto him, We are true men; we are
no spies***

If Joseph used secrets and overcame the tough times, you too can be sure that your solution is finally here. This is the end of your tough times. Joseph never gave up and God saw him through.

FAMINE/TOUGH TIMES #4

In Ruth 1:1-22, we are told of the tough times that Ruth and Naomi experienced and how they overcame.

***1 Now it came to pass in the days when the judges
ruled, that there was a famine in the land. And a certain
man of Bethlehemjudah went to sojourn in the country
of Moab, he, and his wife, and his two sons. 2 And the
name of the man was Elimelech, and the name of his
wife Naomi, and the name of his two sons Mahlon and
Chilion, Ephrathites of Bethlehemjudah. And they came
into the country of Moab, and continued there. 3 And
Elimelech Naomi's husband died; and she was left, and
her two sons.***

***4 And they took them wives of the women of Moab;
the name of the one was Orpah, and the name of the
other Ruth: and they dwelled there about ten years. 5
And Mahlon and Chilion died also both of them; and the
woman was left of her two sons and her husband.***

***6 Then she arose with her daughters in law, that she
might return from the country of Moab: for she had
heard in the country of Moab how that the LORD had
visited his people in giving them bread.***

[7] Wherefore she went forth out of the place where she was, and her two daughters in law with her; and they went on the way to return unto the land of Judah.

[8] And Naomi said unto her two daughters in law, Go, return each to her mother's house: the LORD deal kindly with you, as ye have dealt with the dead, and with me.

[9] The LORD grant you that ye may find rest, each of you in the house of her husband. Then she kissed them; and they lifted up their voice, and wept.

[10] And they said unto her, Surely we will return with thee unto thy people.

[11] And Naomi said, Turn again, my daughters: why will ye go with me? are there yet any more sons in my womb, that they may be your husbands?

[12] Turn again, my daughters, go your way; for I am too old to have an husband. If I should say, I have hope, if I should have an husband also to night, and should also bear sons;

[13] Would ye tarry for them till they were grown? would ye stay for them from having husbands? nay, my daughters; for it grieveth me much for your sakes that the hand of the LORD is gone out against me.

14 And they lifted up their voice, and wept again: and Orpah kissed her mother in law; but Ruth clave unto her.

15 And she said, Behold, thy sister in law is gone back unto her people, and unto her gods: return thou after thy sister in law.

16 And Ruth said, Intreat me not to leave thee, or to return from following after thee: for whither thou goest, I will go; and where thou lodgest, I will lodge: thy people shall be my people, and thy God my God:

17 Where thou diest, will I die, and there will I be buried: the LORD do so to me, and more also, if ought but death part thee and me.

18 When she saw that she was stedfastly minded to go with her, then she left speaking unto her.

19 So they two went until they came to Bethlehem. And it came to pass, when they were come to Bethlehem, that all the city was moved about them, and they said, Is this Naomi?

20 And she said unto them, Call me not Naomi, call me Mara: for the Almighty hath dealt very bitterly with me.

21 I went out full and the LORD hath brought me home again empty: why then call ye me Naomi, seeing the

LORD hath testified against me, and the Almighty hath afflicted me?

[22] So Naomi returned, and Ruth the Moabitess, her daughter in law, with her, which returned out of the country of Moab: and they came to Bethlehem in the beginning of barley harvest.

If Ruth survived her tough times, you will survive it, too. God has a way out already.

FAMINE/TOUGH TIMES #5

Let us read from the book of 2 Kings about Samaria's tough times and how they overcame them.

2 Kings 18 reads,

1 Now it came to pass in the third year of Hoshea son of Elah king of Israel, that Hezekiah the son of Ahaz king of Judah began to reign.

[2] Twenty and five years old was he when he began to reign; and he reigned twenty and nine years in Jerusalem. His mother's name also was Abi, the daughter of Zachariah.

[3] And he did that which was right in the sight of the LORD, according to all that David his father did.

[4] He removed the high places, and brake the images, and cut down the groves, and brake in pieces the brasen serpent that Moses had made: for unto those days the children of Israel did burn incense to it: and he called it Nehushtan.

[5] He trusted in the LORD God of Israel; so that after him was none like him among all the kings of Judah, nor any that were before him.

[6] For he clave to the LORD, and departed not from following him, but kept his commandments, which the LORD commanded Moses.

[7] And the LORD was with him; and he prospered whithersoever he went forth: and he rebelled against the king of Assyria, and served him not.

[8] He smote the Philistines, even unto Gaza, and the borders thereof, from the tower of the watchmen to the fenced city.

[9] And it came to pass in the fourth year of king Hezekiah, which was the seventh year of Hoshea son of Elah king of Israel, that Shalmaneser king of Assyria came up against Samaria, and besieged it.

[10] And at the end of three years they took it: even in the sixth year of Hezekiah, that is in the ninth year of Hoshea king of Israel, Samaria was taken.

[11] And the king of Assyria did carry away Israel unto Assyria, and put them in Halah and in Habor by the river of Gozan, and in the cities of the Medes:

[12] Because they obeyed not the voice of the LORD their God, but transgressed his covenant, and all that Moses the servant of the LORD commanded, and would not hear them, nor do them.

[13] Now in the fourteenth year of king Hezekiah did Sennacherib king of Assyria come up against all the fenced cities of Judah, and took them.

[14] And Hezekiah king of Judah sent to the king of Assyria to Lachish, saying, I have offended; return from me: that which thou puttest on me will I bear. And the king of Assyria appointed unto Hezekiah king of Judah three hundred talents of silver and thirty talents of gold.

[15] And Hezekiah gave him all the silver that was found in the house of the LORD, and in the treasures of the king's house.

[16] At that time did Hezekiah cut off the gold from the doors of the temple of the LORD, and from the pillars

which Hezekiah king of Judah had overlaid, and gave it to the king of Assyria.

[17] ***And the king of Assyria sent Tartan and Rabsaris and Rabshakeh from Lachish to king Hezekiah with a great host against Jerusalem. And they went up and came to Jerusalem. And when they were come up, they came and stood by the conduit of the upper pool, which is in the highway of the fuller's field.***

[18] ***And when they had called to the king, there came out to them Eliakim the son of Hilkiah, which was over the household, and Shebna the scribe, and Joah the son of Asaph the recorder.***

[19] ***And Rabshakeh said unto them, Speak ye now to Hezekiah, Thus saith the great king, the king of Assyria, What confidence is this wherein thou trustest?***

[20] ***Thou sayest, (but they are but vain words,) I have counsel and strength for the war. Now on whom dost thou trust, that thou rebellest against me?***

[21] ***Now, behold, thou trustest upon the staff of this bruised reed, even upon Egypt, on which if a man lean, it will go into his hand, and pierce it: so is Pharaoh king of Egypt unto all that trust on him.***

22 But if ye say unto me, We trust in the LORD our God: is not that he, whose high places and whose altars Hezekiah hath taken away, and hath said to Judah and Jerusalem, Ye shall worship before this altar in Jerusalem?

23 Now therefore, I pray thee, give pledges to my lord the king of Assyria, and I will deliver thee two thousand horses, if thou be able on thy part to set riders upon them.

24 How then wilt thou turn away the face of one captain of the least of my master's servants, and put thy trust on Egypt for chariots and for horsemen?

25 Am I now come up without the LORD against this place to destroy it? The LORD said to me, Go up against this land, and destroy it.

26 Then said Eliakim the son of Hilkiah, and Shebna, and Joah, unto Rabshakeh, Speak, I pray thee, to thy servants in the Syrian language; for we understand it: and talk not with us in the Jews' language in the ears of the people that are on the wall.

27 But Rabshakeh said unto them, Hath my master sent me to thy master, and to thee, to speak these words? hath he not sent me to the men which sit on the

*wall, that they may eat their own dung, and drink their
own piss with you?*

*28 Then Rabshakeh stood and cried with a loud voice
in the Jews' language, and spake, saying, Hear the word
of the great king, the king of Assyria:*

*29 Thus saith the king, Let not Hezekiah deceive you:
for he shall not be able to deliver you out of his hand:*

*30 Neither let Hezekiah make you trust in the LORD,
saying, The LORD will surely deliver us, and this city shall
not be delivered into the hand of the king of Assyria.*

*31 Hearken not to Hezekiah: for thus saith the king of
Assyria, Make an agreement with me by a present, and
come out to me, and then eat ye every man of his own
vine, and every one of his fig tree, and drink ye every one
the waters of his cistern:*

*32 Until I come and take you away to a land like your
own land, a land of corn and wine, a land of bread and
vineyards, a land of oil olive and of honey, that ye may
live, and not die: and hearken not unto Hezekiah, when
he persuadeth you, saying, The LORD will deliver us.*

*33 Hath any of the gods of the nations delivered at all
his land out of the hand of the king of Assyria?*

[34] ***Where are the gods of Hamath, and of Arpad? where are the gods of Sepharvaim, Hena, and Ivah? have they delivered Samaria out of mine hand?***

[35] ***Who are they among all the gods of the countries, that have delivered their country out of mine hand, that the LORD should deliver Jerusalem out of mine hand?***

[36] ***But the people held their peace, and answered him not a word: for the king's commandment was, saying, Answer him not.***

[37] ***Then came Eliakim the son of Hilkiah, which was over the household, and Shebna the scribe, and Joah the son of Asaph the recorder, to Hezekiah with their clothes rent, and told him the words of Rabshakeh.***

2 Kings 6:24-33 reads,

[24] ***And it came to pass after this, that Benhadad king of Syria gathered all his host, and went up, and besieged Samaria.***

[25] ***And there was a great famine in Samaria: and, behold, they besieged it, until an ass's head was sold for fourscore pieces of silver, and the fourth part of a cab of dove's dung for five pieces of silver.***

26 And as the king of Israel was passing by upon the wall, there cried a woman unto him, saying, Help, my lord, O king.

27 And he said, If the LORD do not help thee, whence shall I help thee? out of the barnfloor, or out of the winepress?

28 And the king said unto her, What aileth thee? And she answered, This woman said unto me, Give thy son, that we may eat him to day, and we will eat my son to morrow.

29 So we boiled my son, and did eat him: and I said unto her on the next day, Give thy son, that we may eat him: and she hath hid her son.

30 And it came to pass, when the king heard the words of the woman, that he rent his clothes; and he passed by upon the wall, and the people looked, and, behold, he had sackcloth within upon his flesh.

31 Then he said, God do so and more also to me, if the head of Elisha the son of Shaphat shall stand on him this day.

32 But Elisha sat in his house, and the elders sat with him; and the king sent a man from before him: but ere the messenger came to him, he said to the elders, See

ye how this son of a murderer hath sent to take away mine head? look, when the messenger cometh, shut the door, and hold him fast at the door: is not the sound of his master's feet behind him?

[33] And while he yet talked with them, behold, the messenger came down unto him: and he said, Behold, this evil is of the LORD; what should I wait for the LORD any longer?

2 Kings 7:1-20 reads,

1 Then Elisha said, Hear ye the word of the LORD; Thus saith the LORD, Tomorrow about this time shall a measure of fine flour be sold for a shekel, and two measures of barley for a shekel, in the gate of Samaria.

[2] Then a lord on whose hand the king leaned answered the man of God, and said, Behold, if the LORD would make windows in heaven, might this thing be? And he said, Behold, thou shalt see it with thine eyes, but shalt not eat thereof.

[3] And there were four leprous men at the entering in of the gate: and they said one to another, Why sit we here until we die?

[4] If we say, We will enter into the city, then the famine is in the city, and we shall die there: and if we sit still here, we die also. Now therefore come, and let us fall unto the host of the Syrians: if they save us alive, we shall live; and if they kill us, we shall but die.

[5] And they rose up in the twilight, to go unto the camp of the Syrians: and when they were come to the uttermost part of the camp of Syria, behold, there was no man there.

[6] For the LORD had made the host of the Syrians to hear a noise of chariots, and a noise of horses, even the noise of a great host: and they said one to another, Lo, the king of Israel hath hired against us the kings of the Hittites, and the kings of the Egyptians, to come upon us.

[7] Wherefore they arose and fled in the twilight, and left their tents, and their horses, and their asses, even the camp as it was, and fled for their life.

[8] And when these lepers came to the uttermost part of the camp, they went into one tent, and did eat and drink, and carried thence silver, and gold, and raiment, and went and hid it; and came again, and entered into another tent, and carried thence also, and went and hid it.

[9] Then they said one to another, We do not well: this day is a day of good tidings, and we hold our peace: if we tarry till the morning light, some mischief will come upon us: now therefore come, that we may go and tell the king's household.

[10] So they came and called unto the porter of the city: and they told them, saying, We came to the camp of the Syrians, and, behold, there was no man there, neither voice of man, but horses tied, and asses tied, and the tents as they were.

[11] And he called the porters; and they told it to the king's house within.

[12] And the king arose in the night, and said unto his servants, I will now shew you what the Syrians have done to us. They know that we be hungry; therefore are they gone out of the camp to hide themselves in the field, saying, When they come out of the city, we shall catch them alive, and get into the city.

[13] And one of his servants answered and said, Let some take, I pray thee, five of the horses that remain, which are left in the city, (behold, they are as all the multitude of Israel that are left in it: behold, I say, they

are even as all the multitude of the Israelites that are consumed:) and let us send and see.

14 They took therefore two chariot horses; and the king sent after the host of the Syrians, saying, Go and see.

15 And they went after them unto Jordan: and, lo, all the way was full of garments and vessels, which the Syrians had cast away in their haste. And the messengers returned, and told the king.

16 And the people went out, and spoiled the tents of the Syrians. So a measure of fine flour was sold for a shekel, and two measures of barley for a shekel, according to the word of the LORD.

17 And the king appointed the lord on whose hand he leaned to have the charge of the gate: and the people trode upon him in the gate, and he died, as the man of God had said, who spake when the king came down to him.

18 And it came to pass as the man of God had spoken to the king, saying, Two measures of barley for a shekel, and a measure of fine flour for a shekel, shall be tomorrow about this time in the gate of Samaria:

19 And that lord answered the man of God, and said, Now, behold, if the LORD should make windows in heaven,

might such a thing be? And he said, Behold, thou shalt see it with thine eyes, but shalt not eat thereof.

[20] And so it fell out unto him: for the people trode upon him in the gate, and he died.

God, through the prophet, ended the tough times in Samaria. Therefore, I prophesy the end of your tough times. Study the secrets and apply them now and be free!

FAMINE/TOUGH TIME #6

2 Samuel 21 tells of the tough times that David went through and how he overcame.

1 Then there was a famine in the days of David three years, year after year; and David enquired of the LORD. And the LORD answered, It is for Saul, and for his bloody house, because he slew the Gibeonites.[2] And the king called the Gibeonites, and said unto them; (now the Gibeonites were not of the children of Israel, but of the remnant of the Amorites; and the children of Israel had sworn unto them: and Saul sought to slay them in his zeal to the children of Israel and Judah.)

[3] Wherefore David said unto the Gibeonites, What shall I do for you? and wherewith shall I make the

atonement, that ye may bless the inheritance of the
LORD? 4 And the Gibeonites said unto him, We will have
no silver nor gold of Saul, nor of his house; neither for
us shalt thou kill any man in Israel. And he said, What
ye shall say, that will I do for you.

5 And they answered the king, The man that consumed us, and that devised against us that we should be destroyed from remaining in any of the coasts of Israel,

6 Let seven men of his sons be delivered unto us, and we will hang them up unto the LORD in Gibeah of Saul, whom the LORD did choose. And the king said, I will give them.

7 But the king spared Mephibosheth, the son of Jonathan the son of Saul, because of the LORD's oath that was between them, between David and Jonathan the son of Saul.

8 But the king took the two sons of Rizpah the daughter of Aiah, whom she bare unto Saul, Armoni and Mephibosheth; and the five sons of Michal the daughter of Saul, whom she brought up for Adriel the son of Barzillai the Meholathite:

9 And he delivered them into the hands of the Gibeonites, and they hanged them in the hill before

the LORD: and they fell all seven together, and were put to death in the days of harvest, in the first days, in the beginning of barley harvest.

[10] And Rizpah the daughter of Aiah took sackcloth, and spread it for her upon the rock, from the beginning of harvest until water dropped upon them out of heaven, and suffered neither the birds of the air to rest on them by day, nor the beasts of the field by night.

[11] And it was told David what Rizpah the daughter of Aiah, the concubine of Saul, had done.

[12] And David went and took the bones of Saul and the bones of Jonathan his son from the men of Jabeshgilead, which had stolen them from the street of Bethshan, where the Philistines had hanged them, when the Philistines had slain Saul in Gilboa:

[13] And he brought up from thence the bones of Saul and the bones of Jonathan his son; and they gathered the bones of them that were hanged.

[14] And the bones of Saul and Jonathan his son buried they in the country of Benjamin in Zelah, in the sepulchre of Kish his father: and they performed all that the king commanded. And after that God was intreated for the land.

15 Moreover the Philistines had yet war again with Israel; and David went down, and his servants with him, and fought against the Philistines: and David waxed faint.

16 And Ishbibenob, which was of the sons of the giant, the weight of whose spear weighed three hundred shekels of brass in weight, he being girded with a new sword, thought to have slain David.

*17 But Abishai the son of Zeruiah succoured him, and
smote the Philistine, and killed him. Then the men of
David swore unto him, saying, Thou shalt go no more
out with us to battle, that thou quench not the light of
Israel. 18 And it came to pass after this, that there was
again a battle with the Philistines at Gob: then Sibbechai
the Hushathite slew Saph, which was of the sons of
the giant.*

*19 And there was again a battle in Gob with the
Philistines, where Elhanan the son of Jaareoregim, a
Bethlehemite, slew the brother of Goliath the Gittite,
the staff of whose spear was like a weaver's beam. 20
And there was yet a battle in Gath, where was a man of
great stature, that had on every hand six fingers, and on
every foot six toes, four and twenty in number; and he
also was born to the giant. 21 And when he defied Israel,*

Jonathan the son of Shimeah the brother of David slew him.[22] These four were born to the giant in Gath, and fell by the hand of David, and by the hand of his servants.

If David overcame his tough times, so shall you overcome your tough times, in Jesus' name. All you need to do is to follow step by step, these secrets, and you will be free forever

FAMINE/TOUGH TIMES #7

Job 1 reads,

1 There was a man in the land of Uz, whose name was Job; and that man was perfect and upright, and one that feared God, and eschewed evil.

2 And there were born unto him seven sons and three daughters.

3 His substance also was seven thousand sheep, and three thousand camels, and five hundred yoke of oxen, and five hundred she asses, and a very great household; so that this man was the greatest of all the men of the east.

*4 And his sons went and feasted in their houses,
everyone his day; and sent and called for their three sisters to eat and to drink with them.*

*5 And it was so, when the days of their feasting were
gone about, that Job sent and sanctified them, and
rose up early in the morning, and offered burnt offerings according to the number of them all: for Job said,
It may be that my sons have sinned, and cursed God in
their hearts. Thus did Job continually.*

*6 Now there was a day when the sons of God came
to present themselves before the LORD, and Satan came
also among them.*

*7 And the LORD said unto Satan, Whence comest thou?
Then Satan answered the LORD, and said, From going to
and fro in the earth, and from walking up and down in it.*

*8 And the LORD said unto Satan, Hast thou considered
my servant Job, that there is none like him in the earth,
a perfect and an upright man, one that feareth God, and
escheweth evil?*

*9 Then Satan answered the LORD, and said, Doth Job
fear God for nought?*

*10 Hast not thou made an hedge about him, and about
his house, and about all that he hath on every side? thou*

hast blessed the work of his hands, and his substance is increased in the land.

[11] *But put forth thine hand now, and touch all that he hath, and he will curse thee to thy face.*

[12] *And the LORD said unto Satan, Behold, all that he hath is in thy power; only upon himself put not forth thine hand. So Satan went forth from the presence of the LORD.*

[13] *And there was a day when his sons and his daughters were eating and drinking wine in their eldest brother's house:*

[14] *And there came a messenger unto Job, and said, The oxen were plowing, and the asses feeding beside them:*

[15] *And the Sabeans fell upon them, and took them away; yea, they have slain the servants with the edge of the sword; and I only am escaped alone to tell thee.*

[16] *While he was yet speaking, there came also another, and said, The fire of God is fallen from heaven, and hath burned up the sheep, and the servants, and consumed them; and I only am escaped alone to tell thee.*

[17] *While he was yet speaking, there came also another, and said, The Chaldeans made out three bands, and fell upon the camels, and have carried them away, yea, and*

slain the servants with the edge of the sword; and I only am escaped alone to tell thee.

[18] While he was yet speaking, there came also another, and said, Thy sons and thy daughters were eating and drinking wine in their eldest brother's house:

[19] And, behold, there came a great wind from the wilderness, and smote the four corners of the house, and it fell upon the young men, and they are dead; and I only am escaped alone to tell thee.

[20] Then Job arose, and rent his mantle, and shaved his head, and fell down upon the ground, and worshipped,

[21] And said, Naked came I out of my mother's womb, and naked shall I return thither: the LORD gave, and the LORD hath taken away; blessed be the name of the LORD.

[22] In all this Job sinned not, nor charged God foolishly.

Job 2 reads,

1 Again there was a day when the sons of God came to present themselves before the LORD, and Satan came also among them to present himself before the LORD.

[2] And the LORD said unto Satan, From whence comest thou? And Satan answered the LORD, and said, From going to and fro in the earth, and from walking up and down in it.

3 And the LORD said unto Satan, Hast thou considered my servant Job, that there is none like him in the earth, a perfect and an upright man, one that feareth God, and escheweth evil? and still he holdeth fast his integrity, although thou movedst me against him, to destroy him without cause.

4 And Satan answered the LORD, and said, Skin for skin, yea, all that a man hath will he give for his life.

5 But put forth thine hand now, and touch his bone and his flesh, and he will curse thee to thy face.

6 And the LORD said unto Satan, Behold, he is in thine hand; but save his life.

7 So went Satan forth from the presence of the LORD, and smote Job with sore boils from the sole of his foot unto his crown.

8 And he took him a potsherd to scrape himself withal; and he sat down among the ashes.

9 Then said his wife unto him, Dost thou still retain thine integrity? curse God, and die.

10 But he said unto her, Thou speakest as one of the foolish women speaketh. What? shall we receive good at the hand of God, and shall we not receive evil? In all this did not Job sin with his lips.

11 Now when Job's three friends heard of all this evil that was come upon him, they came every one from his own place; Eliphaz the Temanite, and Bildad the Shuhite, and Zophar the Naamathite: for they had made an appointment together to come to mourn with him and to comfort him.

12 And when they lifted up their eyes afar off, and knew him not, they lifted up their voice, and wept; and they rent every one his mantle, and sprinkled dust upon their heads toward heaven.

13 So they sat down with him upon the ground seven days and seven nights, and none spake a word unto him: for they saw that his grief was very great.

Job 3 reads,

1 After this opened Job his mouth, and cursed his day.

2 And Job spake, and said,

3 Let the day perish wherein I was born, and the night in which it was said, There is a man child conceived.

4 Let that day be darkness; let not God regard it from above, neither let the light shine upon it.

5 Let darkness and the shadow of death stain it; let a cloud dwell upon it; let the blackness of the day terrify it.

6 As for that night, let darkness seize upon it; let it not be joined unto the days of the year, let it not come into the number of the months.

7 Lo, let that night be solitary, let no joyful voice come therein.

8 Let them curse it that curse the day, who are ready to raise up their mourning.

9 Let the stars of the twilight thereof be dark; let it look for light, but have none; neither let it see the dawning of the day:

10 Because it shut not up the doors of my mother's womb, nor hid sorrow from mine eyes.

11 Why died I not from the womb? why did I not give up the ghost when I came out of the belly?

12 Why did the knees prevent me? or why the breasts that I should suck?

13 For now should I have lain still and been quiet, I should have slept: then had I been at rest,

14 With kings and counsellors of the earth, which build desolate places for themselves;

15 Or with princes that had gold, who filled their houses with silver:

*[16] Or as an hidden untimely birth I had not been; as
infants which never saw light.*

*[17] There the wicked cease from troubling; and there
the weary be at rest.*

*[18] There the prisoners rest together; they hear not the
voice of the oppressor.*

*[19] The small and great are there; and the servant is
free from his master.*

*[20] Wherefore is light given to him that is in misery,
and life unto the bitter in soul;*

*[21] Which long for death, but it cometh not; and dig
for it more than for hid treasures;*

*[22] Which rejoice exceedingly, and are glad, when they
can find the grave?*

*[23] Why is light given to a man whose way is hid, and
whom God hath hedged in?*

*[24] For my sighing cometh before I eat, and my roar-
ings are poured out like the waters.*

*[25] For the thing which I greatly feared is come upon
me, and that which I was afraid of is come unto me.*

*[26] I was not in safety, neither had I rest, neither was I
quiet; yet trouble came.*

Job 42 reads,

1 Then Job answered the LORD, and said,

***2 I know that thou canst do everything, and that no
thought can be withholden from thee.***

***3 Who is he that hideth counsel without knowledge?
therefore have I uttered that I understood not; things
too wonderful for me, which I knew not.***

***4 Hear, I beseech thee, and I will speak: I will demand
of thee, and declare thou unto me.***

***5 I have heard of thee by the hearing of the ear: but
now mine eye seeth thee.***

***6 Wherefore I abhor myself, and repent in dust
and ashes.***

***7 And it was so, that after the LORD had spoken these
words unto Job, theLORD said to Eliphaz the Temanite,
My wrath is kindled against thee, and against thy two
friends: for ye have not spoken of me the thing that is
right, as my servant Job hath.***

***8 Therefore take unto you now seven bullocks and
seven rams, and go to my servant Job, and offer up for
yourselves a burnt offering; and my servant Job shall
pray for you: for him will I accept: lest I deal with you***

after your folly, in that ye have not spoken of me the thing which is right, like my servant Job.

[9] So Eliphaz the Temanite and Bildad the Shuhite and Zophar the Naamathite went, and did according as the LORD commanded them: the LORD also accepted Job.

[10] And the LORD turned the captivity of Job, when he prayed for his friends: also the LORD gave Job twice as much as he had before.

[11] Then came there unto him all his brethren, and all his sisters, and all they that had been of his acquaintance before, and did eat bread with him in his house: and they bemoaned him, and comforted him over all the evil that the LORD had brought upon him: every man also gave him a piece of money, and every one an earring of gold.

[12] So the LORD blessed the latter end of Job more than his beginning: for he had fourteen thousand sheep, and six thousand camels, and a thousand yoke of oxen, and a thousand she asses.

[13] He had also seven sons and three daughters.

[14] And he called the name of the first, Jemima; and the name of the second, Kezia; and the name of the third, Kerenhappuch.

[15] ***And in all the land were no women found so fair as the daughters of Job: and their father gave them inheritance among their brethren.***

[16] ***After this lived Job an hundred and forty years, and saw his sons, and his sons' sons, even four generations.***

[17] ***So Job died, being old and full of days.***

If Job overcame his tough times, so shall you victoriously overcome your tough times. Stay faithful to these secrets and apply them to your life.

FAMINE/TOUGH TIMES #8

In Luke 15:11-32, we see the tough times that the prodigal son experienced. How he overcome those tough times is a true testimony that you are coming out of every mess that you are in right now. Expect promotion!

[11] ***And he said, A certain man had two sons:***

[12] ***And the younger of them said to his father, Father, give me the portion of goods that falleth to me. And he divided unto them his living.***

[13] ***And not many days after the younger son gathered all together, and took his journey into a far country, and there wasted his substance with riotous living.***

[14] And when he had spent all, there arose a mighty famine in that land; and he began to be in want.

[15] And he went and joined himself to a citizen of that country; and he sent him into his fields to feed swine.

[16] And he would fain have filled his belly with the husks that the swine did eat: and no man gave unto him.

[17] And when he came to himself, he said, How many hired servants of my father's have bread enough and to spare, and I perish with hunger!

[18] I will arise and go to my father, and will say unto him, Father, I have sinned against heaven, and before thee,

[19] And am no more worthy to be called thy son: make me as one of thy hired servants.

[20] And he arose, and came to his father. But when he was yet a great way off, his father saw him, and had compassion, and ran, and fell on his neck, and kissed him.

[21] And the son said unto him, Father, I have sinned against heaven, and in thy sight, and am no more worthy to be called thy son.

[22] But the father said to his servants, Bring forth the best robe, and put it on him; and put a ring on his hand, and shoes on his feet:

[23] And bring hither the fatted calf, and kill it; and let us eat, and be merry:

[24] For this my son was dead, and is alive again; he was lost, and is found. And they began to be merry.

[25] Now his elder son was in the field: and as he came and drew nigh to the house, he heard music and dancing.

[26] And he called one of the servants, and asked what these things meant.

[27] And he said unto him, Thy brother is come; and thy father hath killed the fatted calf, because he hath received him safe and sound.

[28] And he was angry, and would not go in: therefore came his father out, and intreated him.

[29] And he answering said to his father, Lo, these many years do I serve thee, neither transgressed I at any time thy commandment: and yet thou never gavest me a kid, that I might make merry with my friends:

[30] But as soon as this thy son was come, which hath devoured thy living with harlots, thou hast killed for him the fatted calf.

[31] And he said unto him, Son, thou art ever with me, and all that I have is thine.

[32] It was meet that we should make merry, and be glad: for this thy brother was dead, and is alive again; and was lost, and is found.

These are just a few of the examples of the famine or tough times in the Bible and how they all survived and overcame them. You are next in line. That is why this book is in your hands, to change you and guide you back to the top where you belong. Expect a miracle and a complete turnaround in the name of Jesus.

Chapter 4

WHAT NOT TO DO IN TOUGH TIMES

When going through tough times, there are many things the enemy will throw your way just to confuse and deceive you. Satan will set traps for you and push you to do something that will implicate you the more and that will cause you more tough times.

In this chapter, I want to take you through seven things you should never do in tough times, as directed by the Holy Scriptures. When you know these things and avoid them, you are bound to overcome your tough times. You will also come up and out stronger than before. Every tough time is to build strength and develop character in you by His grace.

According to Romans 8:28, "and we know that all things work together for good to them that love God, to them who are the called according to His purpose." The Bible says all things work together for your good. It means your mistakes will be turned into miracles and your mess will become your message in Jesus' name.

7 Things Never To Do In Tough Times

1) Never Leave God or Break His Covenant.

2 Chronicles 15:1-15; Psalm 78:1-23

2) Never Complain or Murmur.

1 Corinthians 10:10-12; Exodus 12:2, Exodus 17:2

3) Never Confess Negativity.

Numbers 13; Numbers 14:2, 29

4) Never Stop Pressing On.

Philippians 3:7-14

5) Never Stop Sowing or Giving.

Galatians 6:7-10

6) Never Lose Focus.

Matthew 6:19-22

7) Never Ever Give Up.

1 Corinthians 15:57-58; Galatians 6:9

Let us take the above points, one after the other in order of importance, for you to see how many people can miss God and lose focus in tough times. The Bible is filled with a lot of stories and warnings about those who did the wrong things in their tough times.

NEVER LEAVE GOD OR BREAK THE COVENANT.

The first thing to watch out for in tough times is breaking your relationship and fellowship with God. The devil is a covenant breaker, and he will do everything to break your relationship with God. Most people in their tough times stop praying and reading their Bibles, because the enemy will tell them that "stuff didn't work, you don't need to believe in the Bible, God has disappointed you," etc. This is a very dangerous ground that the enemy wants you to tread on. Let us read the story of the children of Israel and how they forgot God in their tough times.

Psalm78 reads,

1 Give ear, O my people, to my law: incline your ears to the words of my mouth.

2 I will open my mouth in a parable: I will utter dark sayings of old:

3 Which we have heard and known, and our fathers have told us.

4 We will not hide them from their children, shewing to the generation to come the praises of the LORD, and his strength, and his wonderful works that he hath done.

5 For he established a testimony in Jacob, and appointed a law in Israel, which he commanded our fathers, that they should make them known to their children:

6 That the generation to come might know them, even the children which should be born; who should arise and declare them to their children:

7 That they might set their hope in God, and not forget the works of God, but keep his commandments:

8 And might not be as their fathers, a stubborn and rebellious generation; a generation that set not their heart aright, and whose spirit was not stedfast with God.

9 The children of Ephraim, being armed, and carrying bows, turned back in the day of battle.

10 They kept not the covenant of God, and refused to walk in his law;

11 And forgot his works, and his wonders that he had shewed them.

*[12] Marvelous things did he in the sight of their fathers,
in the land of Egypt, in the field of Zoan.*

*[13] He divided the sea, and caused them to pass
through; and he made the waters to stand as an heap.*

*[14] In the daytime also he led them with a cloud, and
all the night with a light of fire.*

*[15] He clave the rocks in the wilderness, and gave them
drink as out of the great depths.*

*[16] He brought streams also out of the rock, and caused
waters to run down like rivers.*

*[17] And they sinned yet more against him by provoking
the most High in the wilderness.*

*[18] And they tempted God in their heart by asking
meat for their lust.*

*[19] Yea, they spake against God; they said, Can God
furnish a table in the wilderness?*

*[20] Behold, he smote the rock, that the waters gushed
out, and the streams overflowed; can he give bread
also? can he provide flesh for his people?*

*[21] Therefore the LORD heard this, and was wroth: so
a fire was kindled against Jacob, and anger also came
up against Israel;*

[22] Because they believed not in God, and trusted not in his salvation:

[23] Though he had commanded the clouds from above, and opened the doors of heaven.

As you can see in Psalm 78:9-11, the Bible says that they forgot God and did not keep His covenant. As a result they suffered terribly. You must never leave God or break your covenant with Him. Let us go to 2 Chronicles 15:1-15 to see another example of people who missed God.

2 Chronicles 15:1-15 reads,

1 And the Spirit of God came upon Azariah the son of Oded:

[2] And he went out to meet Asa, and said unto him, Hear ye me, Asa, and all Judah and Benjamin; The LORD is with you, while ye be with him; and if ye seek him, he will be found of you; but if ye forsake him, he will forsake you.

[3] Now for a long season Israel hath been without the true God, and without a teaching priest, and without law.

[4] But when they in their trouble did turn unto the LORD God of Israel, and sought him, he was found of them.

*[5] **And in those times there was no peace to him that***
went out, nor to him that came in, but great vexations
were upon all the inhabitants of the countries.

*[6] **And nation was destroyed of nation, and city of city:***
for God did vex them with all adversity.

*[7] **Be ye strong therefore, and let not your hands be***
weak: for your work shall be rewarded.

*[8] **And when Asa heard these words, and the prophecy***
of Oded the prophet, he took courage, and put away
the abominable idols out of all the land of Judah and
Benjamin, and out of the cities which he had taken from
mount Ephraim, and renewed the altar of the LORD, that
was before the porch of the LORD.

*[9] **And he gathered all Judah and Benjamin, and the***
strangers with them out of Ephraim and Manasseh,
and out of Simeon: for they fell to him out of Israel in
abundance, when they saw that the LORD his God was
with him.

*[10] **So they gathered themselves together at Jerusalem***
in the third month, in the fifteenth year of the reign of Asa.

*[11] **And they offered unto the LORD the same time, of***
the spoil which they had brought, seven hundred oxen
and seven thousand sheep.

[12] And they entered into a covenant to seek the LORD God of their fathers with all their heart and with all their soul;

[13] That whosoever would not seek the LORD God of Israel should be put to death, whether small or great, whether man or woman.

[14] And they sware unto the LORD with a loud voice, and with shouting, and with trumpets, and with cornets.

[15] And all Judah rejoiced at the oath: for they had sworn with all their heart, and sought him with their whole desire; and he was found of them: and the LORD gave them rest round about.

In this story we can see again how during tough times, people can easily miss God. Thank God for the happy ending of this one, especially when they renewed their covenant with God. Verse 15 tells us, "God gave them rest round about." You also will experience rest from all your tough times in Jesus' name as you maintain your walk with God and keep the covenant. Remember, tough times never last!

NEVER COMPLAIN OR MURMUR AGAINST GOD.

Murmuring is a deadly sin that God does not allow. When you complain you remain; where you murmur you mourn. Therefore, never murmur or complain in tough times. It is a deadly, wicked, and terrible thing to do. Let us see the warnings in the Bible about this.

1 Corinthians 10:10-12 reads,

[10] Neither murmur ye, as some of them also murmured, and were destroyed of the destroyer.

[11] Now all these things happened unto them for examples: and they are written for our admonition, upon whom the ends of the world are come.

[12] Wherefore let him that thinketh he standeth take heed lest he fall.

Another example is from Exodus 16:1-25.

1 And they took their journey from Elim, and all the congregation of the children of Israel came unto the wilderness of Sin, which is between Elim and Sinai, on the fifteenth day of the second month after their departing out of the land of Egypt.

[2] And the whole congregation of the children of Israel murmured against Moses and Aaron in the wilderness:

3 ***And the children of Israel said unto them, Would to***
God we had died by the hand of the LORD in the land of
Egypt, when we sat by the flesh pots, and when we did
eat bread to the full; for ye have brought us forth into
this wilderness, to kill this whole assembly with hunger.

4 ***Then said the LORD unto Moses, Behold, I will rain***
bread from heaven for you; and the people shall go out
and gather a certain rate every day, that I may prove
them, whether they will walk in my law, or no.

5 ***And it shall come to pass, that on the sixth day they***
shall prepare that which they bring in; and it shall be
twice as much as they gather daily.

6 ***And Moses and Aaron said unto all the children of***
Israel, At even, then ye shall know that the LORD hath
brought you out from the land of Egypt:

7 ***And in the morning, then ye shall see the glory of***
the LORD; for that he heareth your murmurings against
the LORD: and what are we, that ye murmur against us?

8 ***And Moses said, This shall be, when the LORD shall***
give you in the evening flesh to eat, and in the morning
bread to the full; for that the LORD heareth your mur-
murings which ye murmur against him: and what are

we? your murmurings are not against us, but against
the LORD.

[9] And Moses spake unto Aaron, Say unto all the con-
gregation of the children of Israel, Come near before the
LORD: for he hath heard your murmurings.

[10] And it came to pass, as Aaron spake unto the whole
congregation of the children of Israel, that they looked
toward the wilderness, and, behold, the glory of the
LORD appeared in the cloud.

[11] And the LORD spake unto Moses, saying,

[12] I have heard the murmurings of the children of
Israel: speak unto them, saying, At even ye shall eat flesh,
and in the morning ye shall be filled with bread; and ye
shall know that I am the LORD your God.

[13] And it came to pass, that at even the quails came
up, and covered the camp: and in the morning the dew
lay round about the host.

[14] And when the dew that lay was gone up, behold,
upon the face of the wilderness there lay a small round
thing, as small as the hoar frost on the ground.

[15] And when the children of Israel saw it, they said
one to another, It is manna: for they wist not what it

was. And Moses said unto them, This is the bread which the LORD hath given you to eat.

16 This is the thing which the LORD hath commanded, Gather of it every man according to his eating, an omer for every man, according to the number of your persons; take ye every man for them which are in his tents.

17 And the children of Israel did so, and gathered, some more, some less.

18 And when they did mete it with an omer, he that gathered much had nothing over, and he that gathered little had no lack; they gathered every man according to his eating.

19 And Moses said, Let no man leave of it till the morning.

20 Notwithstanding they hearkened not unto Moses; but some of them left of it until the morning, and it bred worms, and stank: and Moses was wroth with them.

21 And they gathered it every morning, every man according to his eating: and when the sun waxed hot, it melted.

22 And it came to pass, that on the sixth day they gathered twice as much bread, two omers for one man: and all the rulers of the congregation came and told Moses.

[23] And he said unto them, This is that which the LORD hath said, Tomorrow is the rest of the holy sabbath unto the LORD: bake that which ye will bake to day, and seethe that ye will seethe; and that which remaineth over lay up for you to be kept until the morning.

[24] And they laid it up till the morning, as Moses bade: and it did not stink, neither was there any worm therein.

[25] And Moses said, Eat that today; for today is a sabbath unto the LORD: today ye shall not find it in the field.

They still continued to mummer even after that great miracle. Look at Exodus 17:1-8.

1 And all the congregation of the children of Israel journeyed from the wilderness of Sin, after their journeys, according to the commandment of the LORD, and pitched in Rephidim: and there was no water for the people to drink.

[2] Wherefore the people did chide with Moses, and said, Give us water that we may drink. And Moses said unto them, Why chide ye with me? wherefore do ye tempt the LORD?

[3] And the people thirsted there for water; and the people murmured against Moses, and said, Wherefore

is this that thou hast brought us up out of Egypt, to kill us and our children and our cattle with thirst?

[4] And Moses cried unto the LORD, saying, What shall I do unto this people? they be almost ready to stone me.

[5] And the LORD said unto Moses, Go on before the people, and take with thee of the elders of Israel; and thy rod, wherewith thou smotest the river, take in thine hand, and go.

[6] Behold, I will stand before thee there upon the rock in Horeb; and thou shalt smite the rock, and there shall come water out of it, that the people may drink. And Moses did so in the sight of the elders of Israel.

[7] And he called the name of the place Massah, and Meribah, because of the chiding of the children of Israel, and because they tempted the LORD, saying, Is the LORD among us, or not?

[8] Then came Amalek, and fought with Israel in Rephidim.

God will not turn His back on His people in their tough times, but on many occasions, we turn our back against God and murmur and complain. Paul warned against this habit of murmuring and complaining. You are too close to your miracles that you cannot afford to murmur and complain.

Remember, tough times never last. Your miracles are already here, receive them and be blessed. Jesus said, "I will never leave you nor forsake you." He is the helper that you need. Begin to praise God now for His love and power. Stand on His promises; knowing He will never fail you or put you to shame. Never ever give up!

NEVER CONFESS NEGATIVITY.

James 3:1-18 reads,

1 My brethren, be not many masters, knowing that we shall receive the greater condemnation.

2 For in many things we offend all. If any man offend not in word, the same is a perfect man, and able also to bridle the whole body.

3 Behold, we put bits in the horses' mouths, that they may obey us; and we turn about their whole body.

4 Behold also the ships, which though they be so great, and are driven of fierce winds, yet are they turned about with a very small helm, whithersoever the governor listeth.

[5] Even so the tongue is a little member, and boasteth great things. Behold, how great a matter a little fire kindleth!

[6] And the tongue is a fire, a world of iniquity: so is the tongue among our members, that it defileth the whole body, and setteth on fire the course of nature; and it is set on fire of hell.

[7] For every kind of beasts, and of birds, and of serpents, and of things in the sea, is tamed, and hath been tamed of mankind:

[8] But the tongue can no man tame; it is an unruly evil, full of deadly poison.

[9] Therewith bless we God, even the Father; and therewith curse we men, which are made after the similitude of God.

[10] Out of the same mouth proceedeth blessing and cursing. My brethren, these things ought not so to be.

[11] Doth a fountain send forth at the same place sweet water and bitter?

[12] Can the fig tree, my brethren, bear olive berries? either a vine, figs? so can no fountain both yield salt water and fresh.

[13] Who is a wise man and endued with knowledge among you? let him shew out of a good conversation his works with meekness of wisdom.

[14] But if ye have bitter envying and strife in your hearts, glory not, and lie not against the truth.

[15] This wisdom descendeth not from above, but is earthly, sensual, devilish.

[16] For where envying and strife is, there is confusion and every evil work.

[17] But the wisdom that is from above is first pure, then peaceable, gentle, and easy to be intreated, full of mercy and good fruits, without partiality, and without hypocrisy.

[18] And the fruit of righteousness is sown in peace of them that make peace.

Chapter 13 and 14 of the book of Numbers sheds more light on the consequences of negative confessions.

1 And the LORD spake unto Moses, saying,

[2] Send thou men, that they may search the land of Canaan, which I give unto the children of Israel: of every tribe of their fathers shall ye send a man, every one a ruler among them.

***[3] And Moses by the commandment of the LORD sent
them from the wilderness of Paran: all those men were
heads of the children of Israel.***

***[4] And these were their names: of the tribe of Reuben,
Shammua the son of Zaccur.***

[5] Of the tribe of Simeon, Shaphat the son of Hori.

[6] Of the tribe of Judah, Caleb the son of Jephunneh.

[7] Of the tribe of Issachar, Igal the son of Joseph.

[8] Of the tribe of Ephraim, Oshea the son of Nun.

[9] Of the tribe of Benjamin, Palti the son of Raphu.

[10] Of the tribe of Zebulun, Gaddiel the son of Sodi.

***[11] Of the tribe of Joseph, namely, of the tribe of
Manasseh, Gaddi the son of Susi.***

[12] Of the tribe of Dan, Ammiel the son of Gemalli.

[13] Of the tribe of Asher, Sethur the son of Michael.

[14] Of the tribe of Naphtali, Nahbi the son of Vophsi.

[15] Of the tribe of Gad, Geuel the son of Machi.

***[16] These are the names of the men which Moses sent
to spy out the land. And Moses called Oshea the son of
Nun Jehoshua.***

***[17] And Moses sent them to spy out the land of Canaan,
and said unto them, Get you up this way southward, and
go up into the mountain:***

18 And see the land, what it is, and the people that dwelleth therein, whether they be strong or weak, few or many;

19 And what the land is that they dwell in, whether it be good or bad; and what cities they be that they dwell in, whether in tents, or in strong holds;

20 And what the land is, whether it be fat or lean, whether there be wood therein, or not. And be ye of good courage, and bring of the fruit of the land. Now the time was the time of the firstripe grapes.

21 So they went up, and searched the land from the wilderness of Zin unto Rehob, as men come to Hamath.

22 And they ascended by the south, and came unto Hebron; where Ahiman, Sheshai, and Talmai, the children of Anak, were. (Now Hebron was built seven years before Zoan in Egypt.)

23 And they came unto the brook of Eshcol, and cut down from thence a branch with one cluster of grapes, and they bare it between two upon a staff; and they brought of the pomegranates, and of the figs.

24 The place was called the brook Eshcol, because of the cluster of grapes which the children of Israel cut down from thence.

25 And they returned from searching of the land after forty days.

26 And they went and came to Moses, and to Aaron, and to all the congregation of the children of Israel, unto the wilderness of Paran, to Kadesh; and brought back word unto them, and unto all the congregation, and shewed them the fruit of the land.

27 And they told him, and said, We came unto the land whither thou sentest us, and surely it floweth with milk and honey; and this is the fruit of it.

28 Nevertheless the people be strong that dwell in the land, and the cities are walled, and very great: and moreover we saw the children of Anak there.

29 The Amalekites dwell in the land of the south: and the Hittites, and the Jebusites, and the Amorites, dwell in the mountains: and the Canaanites dwell by the sea, and by the coast of Jordan.

30 And Caleb stilled the people before Moses, and said, Let us go up at once, and possess it; for we are well able to overcome it.

31 But the men that went up with him said, We be not able to go up against the people; for they are stronger than we.

[32] And they brought up an evil report of the land which they had searched unto the children of Israel, saying, The land, through which we have gone to search it, is a land that eateth up the inhabitants thereof; and all the people that we saw in it are men of a great stature.

[33] And there we saw the giants, the sons of Anak, which come of the giants: and we were in our own sight as grasshoppers, and so we were in their sight.

Numbers 14

1 And all the congregation lifted up their voice, and cried; and the people wept that night.

[2] And all the children of Israel murmured against Moses and against Aaron: and the whole congregation said unto them, Would God that we had died in the land of Egypt! or would God we had died in this wilderness!

[3] And wherefore hath the LORD brought us unto this land, to fall by the sword, that our wives and our children should be a prey? Were it not better for us to return into Egypt?

[4] And they said one to another, Let us make a captain, and let us return into Egypt.

***5** Then Moses and Aaron fell on their faces before all
the assembly of the congregation of the children of Israel.*

***6** And Joshua the son of Nun, and Caleb the son of
Jephunneh, which were of them that searched the land,
rent their clothes:*

***7** And they spake unto all the company of the children
of Israel, saying, The land, which we passed through to
search it, is an exceeding good land.*

***8** If the LORD delight in us, then he will bring us into
this land, and give it us; a land which floweth with milk
and honey.*

***9** Only rebel not ye against the LORD, neither fear ye
the people of the land; for they are bread for us: their
defence is departed from them, and the LORD is with us:
fear them not.*

***10** But all the congregation bade stone them with
stones. And the glory of the LORD appeared in the tabernacle of the congregation before all the children of Israel.*

***11** And the LORD said unto Moses, How long will
this people provoke me? and how long will it be ere
they believe me, for all the signs which I have shewed
among them?*

12 I will smite them with the pestilence, and disinherit them, and will make of thee a greater nation and mightier than they.

13 And Moses said unto the LORD, Then the Egyptians shall hear it, (for thou broughtest up this people in thy might from among them;)

14 And they will tell it to the inhabitants of this land: for they have heard that thou LORD art among this people, that thou LORD art seen face to face, and that thy cloud standeth over them, and that thou goest before them, by day time in a pillar of a cloud, and in a pillar of fire by night.

15 Now if thou shalt kill all this people as one man, then the nations which have heard the fame of thee will speak, saying,

16 Because the LORD was not able to bring this people into the land which he sware unto them, therefore he hath slain them in the wilderness.

17 And now, I beseech thee, let the power of my lord be great, according as thou hast spoken, saying,

18 The LORD is longsuffering, and of great mercy, forgiving iniquity and transgression, and by no means

clearing the guilty, visiting the iniquity of the fathers upon the children unto the third and fourth generation.

[19] Pardon, I beseech thee, the iniquity of this people according unto the greatness of thy mercy, and as thou hast forgiven this people, from Egypt even until now.

[20] And the LORD said, I have pardoned according to thy word:

[21] But as truly as I live, all the earth shall be filled with the glory of the LORD.

[22] Because all those men which have seen my glory, and my miracles, which I did in Egypt and in the wilderness, and have tempted me now these ten times, and have not hearkened to my voice;

[23] Surely they shall not see the land which I sware unto their fathers, neither shall any of them that provoked me see it:

[24] But my servant Caleb, because he had another spirit with him, and hath followed me fully, him will I bring into the land where into he went; and his seed shall possess it.

[25] (Now the Amalekites and the Canaanites dwelt in the valley.) Tomorrow turn you, and get you into the wilderness by the way of the Red sea.

*26 And the LORD spake unto Moses and unto
Aaron, saying,*

*27 How long shall I bear with this evil congregation,
which murmur against me? I have heard the murmurings
of the children of Israel, which they murmur against me.*

*28 Say unto them, As truly as I live, saith the LORD, as
ye have spoken in mine ears, so will I do to you:*

*29 Your carcases shall fall in this wilderness; and all
that were numbered of you, according to your whole
number, from twenty years old and upward which have
murmured against me.*

*30 Doubtless ye shall not come into the land, con-
cerning which I sware to make you dwell therein, save
Caleb the son of Jephunneh, and Joshua the son of Nun.*

*31 But your little ones, which ye said should be a prey,
them will I bring in, and they shall know the land which
ye have despised.*

*32 But as for you, your carcases, they shall fall in this
wilderness.*

*33 And your children shall wander in the wilderness
forty years, and bear your whoredoms, until your carcases be wasted in the wilderness.*

[34] After the number of the days in which ye searched
the land, even forty days, each day for a year, shall ye
bear your iniquities, even forty years, and ye shall know
my breach of promise.

[35] I the LORD have said, I will surely do it unto all this
evil congregation, that are gathered together against
me: in this wilderness they shall be consumed, and there
they shall die.

[36] And the men, which Moses sent to search the land,
who returned, and made all the congregation to murmur
against him, by bringing up a slander upon the land,

[37] Even those men that did bring up the evil report
upon the land, died by the plague before the LORD.

[38] But Joshua the son of Nun, and Caleb the son of
Jephunneh, which were of the men that went to search
the land, lived still.

[39] And Moses told these sayings unto all the children
of Israel: and the people mourned greatly.

[40] And they rose up early in the morning, and gat
them up into the top of the mountain, saying, Lo, we be
here, and will go up unto the place which the LORD hath
promised: for we have sinned.

***41** And Moses said, Wherefore now do ye transgress the commandment of the LORD? but it shall not prosper.*

***42** Go not up, for the LORD is not among you; that ye be not smitten before your enemies.*

***43** For the Amalekites and the Canaanites are there before you, and ye shall fall by the sword: because ye are turned away from the LORD, therefore the LORD will not be with you.*

***44** But they presumed to go up unto the hill top: nevertheless the ark of the covenant of the LORD, and Moses, departed not out of the camp.*

***45** Then the Amalekites came down, and the Canaanites which dwelt in that hill, and smote them, and discomfited them, even unto Hormah.*

Negative confession is one of the most terrible sicknesses and diseases killing most Christians. It is a tool and weapon from the pit of hell to stop you.

Satan uses this weapon against believers all the time because it is so subtle and silent, but does a lot of damage to your faith and destiny. When you go through tough times, the last thing you want to do is to make a negative confession. Confess positively what the Bible has to say about God, Jesus, the Bible, prayer, and yourself.

We see a lot of examples of many people who ended their blessings and destiny due to negative confessions. What they said and did stopped them. Example number one is Brother Job in the book of Job 1:1-22; according to verse 5, what he feared the most came upon him.

1 There was a man in the land of Uz, whose name was Job; and that man was perfect and upright, and one that feared God, and eschewed evil.

2 And there were born unto him seven sons and three daughters.

3 His substance also was seven thousand sheep, and three thousand camels, and five hundred yoke of oxen, and five hundred she asses, and a very great household; so that this man was the greatest of all the men of the east.

4 And his sons went and feasted in their houses, every one his day; and sent and called for their three sisters to eat and to drink with them.

5 And it was so, when the days of their feasting were gone about, that Job sent and sanctified them, and rose up early in the morning, and offered burnt offerings according to the number of them all: for Job said,

***It may be that my sons have sinned, and cursed God in
their hearts. Thus did Job continually.***

***6 Now there was a day when the sons of God came
to present themselves before the LORD, and Satan came
also among them.***

***7 And the LORD said unto Satan, Whence comest thou?
Then Satan answered the LORD, and said, From going to
and fro in the earth, and from walking up and down in it.***

***8 And the LORD said unto Satan, Hast thou considered
my servant Job, that there is none like him in the earth,
a perfect and an upright man, one that feareth God, and
escheweth evil?***

***9 Then Satan answered the LORD, and said, Doth Job
fear God for nought?***

***10 Hast not thou made an hedge about him, and about
his house, and about all that he hath on every side? thou
hast blessed the work of his hands, and his substance is
increased in the land.***

***11 But put forth thine hand now, and touch all that he
hath, and he will curse thee to thy face.***

***12 And the LORD said unto Satan, Behold, all that he
hath is in thy power; only upon himself put not forth***

thine hand. So Satan went forth from the presence of the LORD.

13 And there was a day when his sons and his daughters were eating and drinking wine in their eldest brother's house:

14 And there came a messenger unto Job, and said, The oxen were plowing, and the asses feeding beside them:

15 And the Sabeans fell upon them, and took them away; yea, they have slain the servants with the edge of the sword; and I only am escaped alone to tell thee.

16 While he was yet speaking, there came also another, and said, The fire of God is fallen from heaven, and hath burned up the sheep, and the servants, and consumed them; and I only am escaped alone to tell thee.

17 While he was yet speaking, there came also another, and said, The Chaldeans made out three bands, and fell upon the camels, and have carried them away, yea, and slain the servants with the edge of the sword; and I only am escaped alone to tell thee.

18 While he was yet speaking, there came also another, and said, Thy sons and thy daughters were eating and drinking wine in their eldest brother's house:

[19] And, behold, there came a great wind from the wilderness, and smote the four corners of the house, and it fell upon the young men, and they are dead; and I only am escaped alone to tell thee.

[20] Then Job arose, and rent his mantle, and shaved his head, and fell down upon the ground, and worshipped,

[21] And said, Naked came I out of my mother's womb, and naked shall I return thither: the LORD gave, and the LORD hath taken away; blessed be the name of the LORD.

[22] In all this Job sinned not, nor charged God foolishly.

As you can see in verse 22, Job refused to confess negatively during his tough times as he had done in verse 5 of the same chapter.

Look at Job 2:9-10.

[9] Then said his wife unto him, Dost thou still retain thine integrity? curse God, and die.

[10] But he said unto her, Thou speakest as one of the foolish women speaketh. What? shall we receive good at the hand of God, and shall we not receive evil? In all this did not Job sin with his lips.

Job here refused to sin against God with his lips knowing full well the penalty and the gravity of negative confession. Job never agreed with his wife about cursing God and dying. You must never speak against God in your tough times.

Speaking against God could mean saying words like, "Oh God why? God, why me? After all my good deeds of righteousness, God, is this how You repay me? Lord, what have I done to deserve this? etc." Satan is behind every trouble, not God. God is not against you, He loves and cares for you. Even when God corrects and chastises us, He does it in love and with mercy. Remember, God is good.

The second example is found in Numbers 13:25-33.

25 And they returned from searching of the land after forty days.

26 And they went and came to Moses, and to Aaron, and to all the congregation of the children of Israel, unto the wilderness of Paran, to Kadesh; and brought back word unto them, and unto all the congregation, and shewed them the fruit of the land.

27 And they told him, and said, We came unto the land whither thou sentest us, and surely it floweth with milk and honey; and this is the fruit of it.

28 Nevertheless the people be strong that dwell in the land, and the cities are walled, and very great: and moreover we saw the children of Anak there.

29 The Amalekites dwell in the land of the south: and the Hittites, and the Jebusites, and the Amorites, dwell in the mountains: and the Canaanites dwell by the sea, and by the coast of Jordan.

30 And Caleb stilled the people before Moses, and said, Let us go up at once, and possess it; for we are well able to overcome it.

31 But the men that went up with him said, We be not able to go up against the people; for they are stronger than we.

32 And they brought up an evil report of the land which they had searched unto the children of Israel, saying, The land, through which we have gone to search it, is a land that eateth up the inhabitants thereof; and all the people that we saw in it are men of a great stature.

33 And there we saw the giants, the sons of Anak, which come of the giants: and we were in our own sight as grasshoppers, and so we were in their sight.

Look at their confessions in verse 33.They said we saw the giants; they never saw the bigness of their God.

They said we are grasshoppers; they confessed failure and defeat. That is what most people do, even today. They never see God but devils, they do not see solutions but sorrows, and they do not see any victory but total defeat. Remember, God is on your side, and you are not alone.

Let's hear from James, one of Jesus' disciples on this matter. James 3:1-12 reads,

3 My brethren, be not many masters, knowing that we shall receive the greater condemnation.

2 For in many things we offend all. If any man offend not in word, the same is a perfect man, and able also to bridle the whole body.

3 Behold, we put bits in the horses' mouths, that they may obey us; and we turn about their whole body.

4 Behold also the ships, which though they be so great, and are driven of fierce winds, yet are they turned about with a very small helm, whithersoever the governor listeth.

5 Even so the tongue is a little member, and boasteth great things. Behold, how great a matter a little fire kindleth!

6 And the tongue is a fire, a world of iniquity: so is the tongue among our members, that it defileth the whole

body, and setteth on fire the course of nature; and it is set on fire of hell.

[7] For every kind of beasts, and of birds, and of serpents, and of things in the sea, is tamed, and hath been tamed of mankind:

[8] But the tongue can no man tame; it is an unruly evil, full of deadly poison.

[9] Therewith bless we God, even the Father; and therewith curse we men, which are made after the similitude of God.

[10] Out of the same mouth proceedeth blessing and cursing. My brethren, these things ought not so to be.

[11] Doth a fountain send forth at the same place sweet water and bitter?

[12] Can the fig tree, my brethren, bear olive berries? either a vine, figs? so can no fountain both yield salt water and fresh.

Look at verses 8-10 again and see the warnings from James to believers. You cannot speak good and evil at the same time. You cannot bless and curse at the same time. James finally said this ought not to be so. Remember to never confess negative in tough times.

NEVER STOP PRESSSING ON.

When going through tough times, the first thing the devil tells you to do is to stop pressing on. He tells you to throw in the towel, quit, turn back, that it is not worth trying anymore; that you have failed and should not waste time pushing on. However, I tell you, in the name of Jesus Christ, from my experience and story to press on.

It is when you feel like quitting and giving up that you are commanded to press on. You are too close now to give up. You have come too far to turn back now–take one more step, shoot one more time, pray one more time. You must not stop pressing on. Look at the example of Paul in the Bible.

Philippians 3:7-17 reads,

[7] ***But what things were gain to me, those I counted loss for Christ.***

[8] ***Yea doubtless, and I count all things but loss for the excellency of the knowledge of Christ Jesus my Lord: for whom I have suffered the loss of all things, and do count them but dung, that I may win Christ,***

[9] ***And be found in him, not having mine own righteousness, which is of the law, but that which is through***

the faith of Christ, the righteousness which is of God by faith:

[10] That I may know him, and the power of his resur-
rection, and the fellowship of his sufferings, being made conformable unto his death;

[11] If by any means I might attain unto the resurrection of the dead.

[12] Not as though I had already attained, either were already perfect: but I follow after, if that I may appre-
hend that for which also I am apprehended of Christ Jesus.

[13] Brethren, I count not myself to have apprehended: but this one thing I do, forgetting those things which are behind, and reaching forth unto those things which are before,

[14] I press toward the mark for the prize of the high calling of God in Christ Jesus.

[15] Let us therefore, as many as be perfect, be thus minded: and if in anything ye be otherwise minded, God shall reveal even this unto you.

[16] Nevertheless, whereto we have already attained, let us walk by the same rule, let us mind the same thing.

[17] Brethren, be followers together of me, and mark them which walk so as ye have us for an ensample.

Paul says in verse 14, "One thing I do is to press toward the mark of the prize in Jesus Christ." He never stopped pressing on. My friend, do not stop pressing on. Look at the example of our father Abraham and Sarah.

Romans 4:17-25 reads,

> [17] ***(As it is written, I have made thee a father of many nations,) before him whom he believed, even God, who quickeneth the dead, and calleth those things which be not as though they were.***
>
> [18] ***Who against hope believed in hope, that he might become the father of many nations, according to that which was spoken, So shall thy seed be.***
>
> [19] ***And being not weak in faith, he considered not his own body now dead, when he was about an hundred years old, neither yet the deadness of Sarah's womb:***
>
> [20] ***He staggered not at the promise of God through unbelief; but was strong in faith, giving glory to God;***
>
> [21] ***And being fully persuaded that, what he had promised, he was able also to perform.***
>
> [22] ***And therefore it was imputed to him for righteousness.***
>
> [23] ***Now it was not written for his sake alone, that it was imputed to him;***

[24] But for us also, to whom it shall be imputed, if we believe on him that raised up Jesus our Lord from the dead;

[25] Who was delivered for our offences, and was raised again for our justification.

Verse 19 says Abraham was not weak in faith, but pressed on to receive the promises. You must press on through these tough times. Abraham and Sarah pressed on; so you must press on, no matter the pain or pressure. The prize is better and bigger than the pain. So press on!

NEVER STOP SOWING OR GIVING.

The last thing you will want to do in tough times is to stop sowing or giving. Giving is living and living is giving. To stop sowing is to stop harvesting. No seed, no harvest, no planting, no reaping. It is the law that no one can break. God set this law from the foundation of the world. If all the farmers in the world stopped sowing or planting, the whole world will collapse; hunger and death will be everywhere because of lack of food. Sowing is the only way to keep feeding the world. Sowing and reaping.

GIVING AND RECEIVING

Satan's best tool is to stop you from sowing or giving in tough times, so he can kill you permanently. He wants to lock you in and frustrate you by whispering into your ears and mind, "Stop giving, things are tough." However, the Bible teaches the opposite. It is when things are tough, that we are commanded to give and sow so God can open up more doors. The farmer plants and sows because he needs new and more crops. Therefore, no matter the tough times, farmers and believers never stop sowing. Let us study a couple of scriptures to see the reality of this.

Galatians 6:7-10 reads,

7 Be not deceived; God is not mocked: for whatsoever a man soweth, that shall he also reap.

8 For he that soweth to his flesh shall of the flesh reap corruption; but he that soweth to the Spirit shall of the Spirit reap life everlasting.

9 And let us not be weary in well doing: for in due season we shall reap, if we faint not.

10 As we have therefore opportunity, let us do good unto all men, especially unto them who are of the household of faith.

Ecclesiastes 11:1-6 reads,

1 Cast thy bread upon the waters: for thou shalt find it after many days.

2 Give a portion to seven, and also to eight; for thou knowest not what evil shall be upon the earth.

3 If the clouds be full of rain, they empty themselves upon the earth: and if the tree fall toward the south, or toward the north, in the place where the tree falleth, there it shall be.

4 He that observeth the wind shall not sow; and he that regardeth the clouds shall not reap.

5 As thou knowest not what is the way of the spirit, nor how the bones do grow in the womb of her that is with child: even so thou knowest not the works of God who maketh all.

6 In the morning sow thy seed, and in the evening withhold not thine hand: for thou knowest not whether shall prosper, either this or that, or whether they both shall be alike good.

Luke 6:38 reads,

38 Give, and it shall be given unto you; good measure, pressed down, and shaken together, and running

over, shall men give into your bosom. For with the same measure that ye mete withal it shall be measured to you again.

Genesis 8:22 reads,

[22] ***While the earth remaineth, seedtime and harvest, and cold and heat, and summer and winter, and day and night shall not cease.***

Let us look at a favorite story in the Bible; the story of the widow who gave her last money. Jesus commended her faith for giving her widow's mite in her tough times. You can learn from her.

Mark 12:41-44 reads,

[41] ***And Jesus sat over against the treasury, and beheld how the people cast money into the treasury: and many that were rich cast in much.***

[42] ***And there came a certain poor widow, and she threw in two mites, which make a farthing.***

[43] ***And he called unto him his disciples, and saith unto them, Verily I say unto you, That this poor widow hath cast more in, than all they which have cast into the treasury:***

[44] ***For all they did cast in of their abundance; but she of her want did cast in all that she had.***

This woman was going through a major tough time in her life. There were so many things against her, but she was still sowing and giving; this is a major key to overcoming tough times. She had five major challenges against her that would have been a good excuses to stop giving, but she made the right choice.

Let's look at her challenges:

- She was a widow (no husband).
- She had no money.
- She had no food.
- She had no source of income.
- She was giving her last money away.

This was a very bad and tough situation, but she made the right move and Jesus said, she gave the greatest gift and her seed became special to God and man. The harvest continues until today. You can do the same. Never stop giving in tough times.

NEVER LOSE FOCUS.

When you lose focus in life, you lose everything. Tough times come against you for one reason and that is just to break your focus. Satan knows that when he breaks your focus, he has defeated you already. According to Mike Murdock, the reason why people fail in life is because of broken focus. Broken focus is dangerous and deadly to your faith. In tough times it is easy to lose your focus, without the help of God. You must maintain your focus.

Matthew 6:22-23 reads,

22 The light of the body is the eye: if therefore thine eye be single, thy whole body shall be full of light.

23 But if thine eye be evil, thy whole body shall be full of darkness. If therefore the light that is in thee be darkness, how great is that darkness!

There are three major areas you must maintain focus in tough times, according to the Holy Scriptures.

- Focus on God, your only helper.
- Focus on the solution and not the problem.
- Focus on where you are going and not where you are.

Let us look at the story of Peter and the Master in Matthew 14:22-33. This is a perfect example about this issue on focus.

22 And straightway Jesus constrained his disciples to get into a ship, and to go before him unto the other side, while he sent the multitudes away.

23 And when he had sent the multitudes away, he went up into a mountain apart to pray: and when the evening was come, he was there alone.

24 But the ship was now in the midst of the sea, tossed with waves: for the wind was contrary.

25 And in the fourth watch of the night Jesus went unto them, walking on the sea.

26 And when the disciples saw him walking on the sea, they were troubled, saying, It is a spirit; and they cried out for fear.

27 But straightway Jesus spake unto them, saying, Be of good cheer; it is I; be not afraid.

28 And Peter answered him and said, Lord, if it be thou, bid me come unto thee on the water.

29 And he said, Come. And when Peter was come down out of the ship, he walked on the water, to go to Jesus.

30 But when he saw the wind boisterous, he was afraid;
and beginning to sink, he cried, saying, Lord, save me.
31 And immediately Jesus stretched forth his hand,
and caught him, and said unto him, O thou of little faith,
wherefore didst thou doubt?
32 And when they were come into the ship, the
wind ceased.
33 Then they that were in the ship came and worshipped him, saying, Of a truth thou art the Son of God.

In verse 30, the Bible says in that tough time Peter lost focus. When he saw the wind, his focus changed from Jesus to the wind and from walking on the water to sinking in the same water. That may be your story, too. Perhaps you came from success to failure; from winning to defeat because of lack of focus. Stay focused no matter what you are going through. God is there in the midst of it, but you must focus on Him. The Bible encourages us to focus on Jesus, our Lord, Master, Savior, Deliverer, and Commander-in-Chief.

Hebrews 12:1-3

1 Wherefore seeing we also are compassed about with so great a cloud of witnesses, let us lay aside every

weight, and the sin which doth so easily beset us, and let us run with patience the race that is set before us,

2 Looking unto Jesus the author and finisher of our faith; who for the joy that was set before him endured the cross, despising the shame, and is set down at the right hand of the throne of God.

3 For consider him that endured such contradiction of sinners against himself, lest ye be wearied and faint in your minds.

You cannot focus on Jesus and Satan at the same time. The Bible says you cannot serve two masters. God is with you. Focus on Him alone.

2 Corinthians 4:16-18 reads,

16 For which cause we faint not; but though our outward man perish, yet the inward man is renewed day by day.

17 For our light affliction, which is but for a moment, worketh for us a far more exceeding and eternal weight of glory;

18 While we look not at the things which are seen, but at the things which are not seen: for the things which

are seen are temporal; but the things which are not seen are eternal.

Paul, in his letter to the believers in Corinth, told them not to look at the things we see but at the things which are not seen. In other words, focus on the solution and not the trouble; focus on answers and not questions; focus on winning and not failing, and encourage yourself in the name of Jesus to focus on victory. Jesus is the way maker; He will never forsake you or fail you. Your tough times will never last, and your God will see you through.

I have personally been through hell and back, but God is faithful. I am here today, because of His love and mercy and my focus on Him and His powerful promises.

NEVER EVER GIVE UP.

This is my favorite of all the seven things never to do in tough times. Never ever give up or quit. Do not give up of God, yourself, destiny, spouse, family, church, work, business, and dreams.

Remember, tough times never last. You are on the verge of a major breakthrough that will last a life time, so press on.

There are eight basic things you must not give up in your tough times; hold on to them and the rest will be history.

NINE THINGS NEVER TO GIVE UP

1. Your prayer life
2. Your study life
3. Your faith life
4. Your marriage
5. Your friendships
6. Your obedience
7. Your righteousness
8. Your dreams/goals
9. Your destiny/birthright

Look at the command of God to you from the following scriptures and really take them seriously. I have lived by these commands, hence the book you are reading. Your story is the next one in Jesus' name.

Romans 8:35-39

35 ***Who shall separate us from the love of Christ? shall tribulation, or distress, or persecution, or famine, or***

nakedness, or peril, or sword? [36] As it is written, For thy
sake we are killed all the day long; we are accounted as
sheep for the slaughter.[37] Nay, in all these things we are
more than conquerors through him that loved us.[38] For
I am persuaded, that neither death, nor life, nor angels, nor principalities, nor powers, nor things present, nor things to come,

[39] Nor height, nor depth, nor any other creature, shall be able to separate us from the love of God, which is in Christ Jesus our Lord.

The next example is the advice of Paul to the Corinthians and to you.

2 Corinthians 4:8-12 reads,

[8] We are troubled on every side, yet not distressed;
we are perplexed, but not in despair; [9] Persecuted, but
not forsaken; cast down, but not destroyed;[10] Always
bearing about in the body the dying of the Lord Jesus, that the life also of Jesus might be made manifest in
our body. [11] For we which live are always delivered unto
death for Jesus' sake, that the life also of Jesus might be
made manifest in our mortal flesh. [12] So then death wor-
keth in us, but life in you.

We will further hear from Paul as he speaks to the church at Galatia and to you right now.

Galatians 6:9-10 reads,

[9] ***And let us not be weary in well doing: for in due season we shall reap, if we faint not.***

[10] ***As we have therefore opportunity, let us do good unto all men, especially unto them who are of the household of faith.***

Chapter 5

HOW TO OVERCOME TOUGH TIMES– THE WAY OUT

The Bible says we are overcomers, and that whosoever is born of God overcomes the world. The "world" meaning, the system of this earth realm and the ruler of the sense world is Satan. To overcome means to overcome Satan and all his demons.

Luke 10:19 reads,

19 Behold, I give unto you power to tread on serpents and scorpions, and over all the power of the enemy: and nothing shall by any means hurt you.

1 John 4:4-6 reads,

4 Ye are of God, little children, and have overcome them: because greater is he that is in you, than he that is in the world.

5 They are of the world: therefore speak they of the world, and the world heareth them.

6 We are of God: he that knoweth God heareth us; he that is not of God heareth not us. Hereby know we the spirit of truth, and the spirit of error.

1 John 5:1-5 reads,

1 Whosoever believeth that Jesus is the Christ is born of God: and every one that loveth him that begat loveth him also that is begotten of him.

2 By this we know that we love the children of God,
when we love God, and keep his commandments. 3 For
this is the love of God, that we keep his commandments:
and his commandments are not grievous. 4 For whatso-
ever is born of God overcometh the world: and this is the
victory that overcometh the world, even our faith. 5 Who
is he that overcometh the world, but he that believeth
that Jesus is the Son of God?

Revelation 12:11 reads,

[1] ***And they overcame him by the blood of the Lamb, and by the word of their testimony; and they loved not their lives unto the death.***

To overcome something is to conquer it completely; to win against it and be victorious; to "come-over" anything that is standing in your way – be it giants, mountains or spirits. To overcome is to defeat anything. An over comer overcomes all challenges in life. God calls us overcomers, and that is who we are. The Father has given us every ability and authority to overcome Satan and his cohorts. Get ready to take territories for Jesus Christ; you are one of the end time movers and shakers of nations.

With this knowledge and tool in your hands, the devil and demons are in trouble. Rejoice today; you are an overcome in Jesus Christ. Nothing can defeat you.

God spoke to me clearly, to go and raise an army of overcomers that will never be defeated, hence this book.

Revelation 21:7

[7] ***He that overcometh shall inherit all things; and I will be his God, and he shall be my son.***

REVELATION – THE WAY OUT

One of the basic and most important truths in overcoming tough times is revelation. You must know and have this revelation that tough times never last. You must know that your tough times are for a reason. You must know that your tough times are just for a season. No matter how long it takes, it is for a season.

Ecclesiastes 3:1-4 reads,

1 To everything there is a season, and a time to every purpose under the heaven:2 A time to be born, and a time to die; a time to plant, and a time to pluck up that which is planted;3 A time to kill, and a time to heal; a time to break down, and a time to build up;4 A time to weep, and a time to laugh; a time to mourn, and a time to dance;

From this scripture, we see clearly that there is time for everything. Whatever you are going through cannot last forever. There is a time limit to it. You can shorten it or prolong it by what you do, say, and believe. Your time is now.

The second revelation you must have is that there is always a way out of all tough times. There is a way out of all your crises and troubles. God promised to make a way in the wilderness for you and make a way where there is no way. He is the way maker. Believe Him today!

Join me now as we take a journey on some of the things to do to overcome your tough times.

Isaiah 5:8-11 reads,

[8] ***Woe unto them that join house to house, that lay field to field, till there be no place, that they may be placed alone in the midst of the earth!*** [9] ***In mine ears said the LORD of hosts, Of a truth many houses shall be desolate, even great and fair, without inhabitant.*** [10] ***Yea, ten acres of vineyard shall yield one bath, and the seed of an homer shall yield an ephah.*** [11] ***Woe unto them that rise up early in the morning, that they may follow strong drink; that continue until night, till wine inflame them!***

1 Corinthians 10:13 reads,

13 There hath no temptation taken you but such as is common to man: but God is faithful, who will not suffer you to be tempted above that ye are able; but will with

the temptation also make a way to escape, that ye may be able to bear it.

TO OVERCOME TOUGH TIMES…

- Please God.
- Obey God.
- Love God.
- Serve God.
- Honor God.
- Connect to Jesus – Pursue His power.
- Practice His principles.
- Have purpose for living.
- Partner with other.
- Persist.
- Patiently go through the process.
- Praise your way out.

Let us study the above steps carefully, as we believe the power of God to help you overcome all tough times. No matter what kind of tough times you are facing, this is the way out. It is tested and proven.

John 14:1-6 reads,

1 Let not your heart be troubled: ye believe in God, believe also in me.[2] In my Father's house are many mansions: if it were not so, I would have told you. I go to prepare a place for you.

[3] And if I go and prepare a place for you, I will come again, and receive you unto myself; that where I am, there ye may be also.

[4] And whither I go ye know, and the way ye know.

[5] Thomas saith unto him, Lord, we know not whither thou goest; and how can we know the way?

[6] Jesus saith unto him, I am the way, the truth, and the life: no man cometh unto the Father, but by me.

Let us follow these steps, and I assure you that you are sure of stepping out all frustrations, pains, and problems.

STEP 1 – PLEASE GOD.

You were designed and created to please God. When you please God, all hell will bow to you.

Revelation 4:11 reads,

[11] Thou art worthy, O Lord, to receive glory and honor and power: for thou hast created all things, and for thy pleasure they are and were created.

Proverbs 16:7 reads,

[7] When a man's ways please the LORD, he maketh even his enemies to be at peace with him.

Colossians 1:10 reads,

[10] That ye might walk worthy of the Lord unto all pleasing, being fruitful in every good work, and increasing in the knowledge of God.

STEP 2 – OBEY GOD.

The greatest thing God demands and requires from man is obedience. God wants to be obeyed. If you choose to obey God, all will be well with you.

Isaiah 1:19-20 reads,

[19] If ye be willing and obedient, ye shall eat the good of the land:

[20] But if ye refuse and rebel, ye shall be devoured with the sword: for the mouth of the LORD hath spoken it.

Jeremiah 7 reads,

1 The word that came to Jeremiah from the LORD, saying,

[2] Stand in the gate of the LORD's house, and proclaim there this word, and say, Hear the word of the LORD, all ye of Judah, that enter in at these gates to worship the LORD.

[3] Thus saith the LORD of hosts, the God of Israel, Amend your ways and your doings, and I will cause you to dwell in this place.

[4] Trust ye not in lying words, saying, The temple of the LORD, The temple of the LORD, The temple of the LORD, are these.

[5] For if ye thoroughly amend your ways and your doings; if ye thoroughly execute judgment between a man and his neighbor;

[6] If ye oppress not the stranger, the fatherless, and the widow, and shed not innocent blood in this place, neither walk after other gods to your hurt:

7 Then will I cause you to dwell in this place, in the land that I gave to your fathers, for ever and ever.

8 Behold, ye trust in lying words that cannot profit.

9 Will ye steal, murder, and commit adultery, and swear falsely, and burn incense unto Baal, and walk after other gods whom ye know not;

10 And come and stand before me in this house, which is called by my name, and say, We are delivered to do all these abominations?

11 Is this house, which is called by my name, become a den of robbers in your eyes? Behold, even I have seen it, saith the LORD.

12 But go ye now unto my place which was in Shiloh, where I set my name at the first, and see what I did to it for the wickedness of my people Israel.

13 And now, because ye have done all these works, saith the LORD, and I spake unto you, rising up early and speaking, but ye heard not; and I called you, but ye answered not;

14 Therefore will I do unto this house, which is called by my name, wherein ye trust, and unto the place which I gave to you and to your fathers, as I have done to Shiloh.

[15] And I will cast you out of my sight, as I have cast out all your brethren, even the whole seed of Ephraim.

[16] Therefore pray not thou for this people, neither lift up cry nor prayer for them, neither make intercession to me: for I will not hear thee.

[17] Seest thou not what they do in the cities of Judah and in the streets of Jerusalem?

[18] The children gather wood, and the fathers kindle the fire, and the women knead their dough, to make cakes to the queen of heaven, and to pour out drink offerings unto other gods, that they may provoke me to anger.

[19] Do they provoke me to anger? saith the LORD: do they not provoke themselves to the confusion of their own faces?

[20] Therefore thus saith the Lord GOD; Behold, mine anger and my fury shall be poured out upon this place, upon man, and upon beast, and upon the trees of the field, and upon the fruit of the ground; and it shall burn, and shall not be quenched.

[21] Thus saith the LORD of hosts, the God of Israel; Put your burnt offerings unto your sacrifices, and eat flesh.

[22] For I spake not unto your fathers, nor commanded them in the day that I brought them out of the land of Egypt, concerning burnt offerings or sacrifices:

[23] But this thing commanded I them, saying, Obey my voice, and I will be your God, and ye shall be my people: and walk ye in all the ways that I have commanded you, that it may be well unto you.

[24] But they hearkened not, nor inclined their ear, but walked in the counsels and in the imagination of their evil heart, and went backward, and not forward.

[25] Since the day that your fathers came forth out of the land of Egypt unto this day I have even sent unto you all my servants the prophets, daily rising up early and sending them:

[26] Yet they hearkened not unto me, nor inclined their ear, but hardened their neck: they did worse than their fathers.

[27] Therefore thou shalt speak all these words unto them; but they will not hearken to thee: thou shalt also call unto them; but they will not answer thee.

[28] But thou shalt say unto them, This is a nation that obeyeth not the voice of the LORD their God, nor

receiveth correction: truth is perished, and is cut off from their mouth.

[29] Cut off thine hair, O Jerusalem, and cast it away, and take up a lamentation on high places; for the LORD hath rejected and forsaken the generation of his wrath.

[30] For the children of Judah have done evil in my sight, saith the LORD: they have set their abominations in the house which is called by my name, to pollute it.

[31] And they have built the high places of Tophet, which is in the valley of the son of Hinnom, to burn their sons and their daughters in the fire; which I commanded them not, neither came it into my heart.

[32] Therefore, behold, the days come, saith the LORD, that it shall no more be called Tophet, nor the valley of the son of Hinnom, but the valley of slaughter: for they shall bury in Tophet, till there be no place.

[33] And the carcases of this people shall be meat for the fowls of the heaven, and for the beasts of the earth; and none shall fray them away.

[34] Then will I cause to cease from the cities of Judah, and from the streets of Jerusalem, the voice of mirth, and the voice of gladness, the voice of the bridegroom, and the voice of the bride: for the land :

Job 36:11-12 reads,

[11] ***If they obey and serve him, they shall spend their days in prosperity, and their years in pleasures.***

[12] ***But if they obey not, they shall perish by the sword, and they shall die without knowledge.***

STEP 3 – LOVE GOD.

Unconditional love for God is what Jesus taught. When He was asked about the greatest commandment in the Bible, His answer was shocking to the Sadducees and Pharisees. They thought they loved God, only to find out that what they called love or defined as love, was not how God, the king of love, defined it. Unconditional love for God is a must even in your tough times.

Matthew 22:36-40 reads,

[36] ***Master, which is the great commandment in the law?***

[37] ***Jesus said unto him, Thou shalt love the Lord thy God with all thy heart, and with all thy soul, and with all thy mind.***[38] ***This is the first and great commandment.***

***39** And the second is like unto it, Thou shalt love thy neighbour as thyself.*

***40** On these two commandments hang all the law and the prophets.*

Romans 8:28 reads,

***28** And we know that all things work together for good to them that love God, to them who are the called according to his purpose.*

1 Corinthians 2:9-12 reads.

***9** But as it is written, Eye hath not seen, nor ear heard, neither have entered into the heart of man, the things which God hath prepared for them that love him.*

***10** But God hath revealed them unto us by his Spirit: for the Spirit searcheth all things, yea, the deep things of God.*

***11** For what man knoweth the things of a man, save the spirit of man which is in him? even so the things of God knoweth no man, but the Spirit of God.*

***12** Now we have received, not the spirit of the world, but the spirit which is of God; that we might know the things that are freely given to us of God.*

STEP 4 – SERVE GOD.

In Matthew 6:24, Jesus said you cannot serve God and mammon. Your service to God must be unquestionable. You must serve God with complete dedication and with no reservations. You were created to serve God. Your salvation will not be complete without your service. Jesus declared He did not come to be served, but to serve others. Your joy is in serving God and man.

Matthew 6:24 reads.

[24] ***No man can serve two masters: for either he will hate the one, and love the other; or else he will hold to the one, and despise the other. Ye cannot serve God and mammon.***

Matthew 20:28 reads,

[28] ***Even as the Son of man came not to be ministered unto, but to minister, and to give his life a ransom for many***

Exodus 23:25 reads,

[25] And ye shall serve the LORD your God, and he shall bless thy bread, and thy water; and I will take sickness away from the midst of thee.

Joshua 24:15 reads,

[15] And if it seem evil unto you to serve the LORD, choose you this day whom ye will serve; whether the gods which your fathers served that were on the other side of the flood, or the gods of the Amorites, in whose land ye dwell: but as for me and my house, we will serve the LORD.

Job 36:11 reads,

[11] If they obey and serve him, they shall spend their days in prosperity, and their years in pleasures.

STEP 5 – HONOR GOD.

The Lord God says, "Him that honors Me, I will honor." When you honor God, He will see to it that all tough times bow to you. We are commanded to honor God at all times.

1 Samuel 2:20 reads,

***20** And Eli blessed Elkanah and his wife, and said, The LORD give thee seed of this woman for the loan which is lent to the LORD. And they went unto their own home.*

Let us also look at chapter 1 and 2 of the book of Haggai.

Haggai 1 reads,

***1** In the second year of Darius the king, in the sixth month, in the first day of the month, came the word of the LORD by Haggai the prophet unto Zerubbabel the son of Shealtiel, governor of Judah, and to Joshua the son of Josedech, the high priest, saying,*

***2** Thus speaketh the LORD of hosts, saying, This people say, The time is not come, the time that the LORD's house should be built.*

***3** Then came the word of the LORD by Haggai the prophet, saying,*

***4** Is it time for you, O ye, to dwell in your cieled houses, and this house lie waste?*

***5** Now therefore thus saith the LORD of hosts; Consider your ways.*

***6** Ye have sown much, and bring in little; ye eat, but ye have not enough; ye drink, but ye are not filled with* *drink; ye clothe you, but there is none warm; and he that earneth wages earneth wages to put it into a bag with holes.*

7 Thus saith the LORD of hosts; Consider your ways.

8 Go up to the mountain, and bring wood, and build the house; and I will take pleasure in it, and I will be glorified, saith the LORD.

9 Ye looked for much, and, lo it came to little; and when ye brought it home, I did blow upon it. Why? saith the LORD of hosts. Because of mine house that is waste, and ye run every man unto his own house.

10 Therefore the heaven over you is stayed from dew, and the earth is stayed from her fruit.

11 And I called for a drought upon the land, and upon the mountains, and upon the corn, and upon the new wine, and upon the oil, and upon that which the ground bringeth forth, and upon men, and upon cattle, and upon all the labour of the hands.

12 Then Zerubbabel the son of Shealtiel, and Joshua the son of Josedech, the high priest, with all the remnant of the people, obeyed the voice of the LORD their God, and the words of Haggai the prophet, as the LORD

their God had sent him, and the people did fear before the LORD.

[13] Then spake Haggai the LORD's messenger in the LORD's message unto the people, saying, I am with you, saith the LORD.

[14] And the LORD stirred up the spirit of Zerubbabel the son of Shealtiel, governor of Judah, and the spirit of Joshua the son of Josedech, the high priest, and the spirit of all the remnant of the people; and they came and did work in the house of the LORD of hosts, their God,

[15] In the four and twentieth day of the sixth month, in the second year of Darius the king.

Haggai 2 reads,

2 In the seventh month, in the one and twentieth day of the month, came the word of the LORD by the prophet Haggai, saying,

[2] Speak now to Zerubbabel the son of Shealtiel, governor of Judah, and to Joshua the son of Josedech, the high priest, and to the residue of the people, saying,

[3] Who is left among you that saw this house in her first glory? and how do ye see it now? is it not in your eyes in comparison of it as nothing?

**4 Yet now be strong, O Zerubbabel, saith the LORD;
and be strong, O Joshua, son of Josedech, the high priest;
and be strong, all ye people of the land, saith the LORD,
and work: for I am with you, saith the LORD of hosts:**

**5 According to the word that I covenanted with you
when ye came out of Egypt, so my spirit remaineth
among you: fear ye not.**

**6 For thus saith the LORD of hosts; Yet once, it is a little
while, and I will shake the heavens, and the earth, and
the sea, and the dry land;**

**7 And I will shake all nations, and the desire of all
nations shall come: and I will fill this house with glory,
saith the LORD of hosts.**

**8 The silver is mine, and the gold is mine, saith the
LORD of hosts.**

**9 The glory of this latter house shall be greater than
of the former, saith the LORD of hosts: and in this place
will I give peace, saith the LORD of hosts.**

**10 In the four and twentieth day of the ninth month,
in the second year of Darius, came the word of the LORD
by Haggai the prophet, saying,**

**11 Thus saith the LORD of hosts; Ask now the priests
concerning the law, saying,**

**[12] If one bear holy flesh in the skirt of his garment, and
with his skirt do touch bread, or pottage, or wine, or oil,
or any meat, shall it be holy? And the priests answered
and said, No.**

**[13] Then said Haggai, If one that is unclean by a dead
body touch any of these, shall it be unclean? And the
priests answered and said, It shall be unclean.**

**[14] Then answered Haggai, and said, So is this people,
and so is this nation before me, saith the LORD; and so
is every work of their hands; and that which they offer
there is unclean.**

**[15] And now, I pray you, consider from this day and
upward, from before a stone was laid upon a stone in
the temple of the LORD:**

**[16] Since those days were, when one came to an heap
of twenty measures, there were but ten: when one came
to the pressfat for to draw out fifty vessels out of the
press, there were but twenty.**

**[17] I smote you with blasting and with mildew and
with hail in all the labours of your hands; yet ye turned
not to me, saith the LORD.**

**[18] Consider now from this day and upward, from the
four and twentieth day of the ninth month, even from**

the day that the foundation of the LORD's temple was laid, consider it.

[19] Is the seed yet in the barn? yea, as yet the vine, and the fig tree, and the pomegranate, and the olive tree, hath not brought forth: from this day will I bless you.

[20] And again the word of the LORD came unto Haggai in the four and twentieth day of the month, saying,

[21] Speak to Zerubbabel, governor of Judah, saying, I will shake the heavens and the earth;

[22] And I will overthrow the throne of kingdoms, and I will destroy the strength of the kingdoms of the heathen; and I will overthrow the chariots, and those that ride in them; and the horses and their riders shall come down, everyone by the sword of his brother.

[23] In that day, saith the LORD of hosts, will I take thee, O Zerubbabel, my servant, the son of Shealtiel, saith the LORD, and will make thee as a signet: for I have chosen thee, saith the LORD of hosts.

Malachi 1 further reinforces the importance of honoring God. Let us read this chapter.

1 The burden of the word of the LORD to Israel by Malachi.

[2] I have loved you, saith the LORD. Yet ye say, Wherein hast thou loved us? Was not Esau Jacob's brother? saith the LORD: yet I loved Jacob,

[3] And I hated Esau, and laid his mountains and his heritage waste for the dragons of the wilderness.

[4] Whereas Edom saith, We are impoverished, but we will return and build the desolate places; thus saith the LORD of hosts, They shall build, but I will throw down; and they shall call them, The border of wickedness, and, The people against whom the LORD hath indignation forever.

[5] And your eyes shall see, and ye shall say, The LORD will be magnified from the border of Israel.

[6] A son honoureth his father, and a servant his master: if then I be a father, where is mine honour? and if I be a master, where is my fear? saith the LORD of hosts unto you, O priests, that despise my name. And ye say, Wherein have we despised thy name?

[7] Ye offer polluted bread upon mine altar; and ye say, Wherein have we polluted thee? In that ye say, The table of the LORD is contemptible.

[8] And if ye offer the blind for sacrifice, is it not evil? and if ye offer the lame and sick, is it not evil? offer it

now unto thy governor; will he be pleased with thee, or accept thy person? saith the LORD of hosts.

[9] And now, I pray you, beseech God that he will be gracious unto us: this hath been by your means: will he regard your persons? saith the LORD of hosts.

[10] Who is there even among you that would shut the doors for nought? neither do ye kindle fire on mine altar for nought. I have no pleasure in you, saith the LORD of hosts, neither will I accept an offering at your hand.

[11] For from the rising of the sun even unto the going down of the same my name shall be great among the Gentiles; and in every place incense shall be offered unto my name, and a pure offering: for my name shall be great among the heathen, saith the LORD of hosts.

[12] But ye have profaned it, in that ye say, The table of the LORD is polluted; and the fruit thereof, even his meat, is contemptible.

[13] Ye said also, Behold, what a weariness is it! and ye have snuffed at it, saith the LORD of hosts; and ye brought that which was torn, and the lame, and the sick; thus ye brought an offering: should I accept this of your hand? saith the LORD.

[14] But cursed be the deceiver, which hath in his flock a male, and voweth, and sacrificeth unto the LORD a corrupt thing: for I am a great King, saith the LORD of hosts, and my name is dreadful among the heathen.

STEP 6 – CONNECT TO JESUS.

You cannot fight alone and you cannot survive without Jesus. He is the way, the truth, and the life. He defeated Satan for you. He is our King, connect to Him today. When you connect to Jesus, all tough times will submit to Him, the King of kings and the Lord of lords. He now lives inside of you. Believe Him.

John 15:1-8 reads,

1 I am the true vine, and my Father is the husbandman.

[2] Every branch in me that beareth not fruit he taketh away: and every branch that beareth fruit, he purgeth it, that it may bring forth more fruit.

[3] Now ye are clean through the word which I have spoken unto you.

[4] Abide in me, and I in you. As the branch cannot bear fruit of itself, except it abide in the vine; no more can ye, except ye abide in me.

[5] I am the vine, ye are the branches: He that abideth in me, and I in him, the same bringeth forth much fruit: for without me ye can do nothing.

[6] If a man abide not in me, he is cast forth as a branch, and is withered; and men gather them, and cast them into the fire, and they are burned.

[7] If ye abide in me, and my words abide in you, ye shall ask what ye will, and it shall be done unto you.

[8] Herein is my Father glorified, that ye bear much fruit; so shall ye be my disciples.

2 Corinthians 5:17 reads,

[17] Therefore if any man be in Christ, he is a new creature: old things are passed away; behold, all things are become new.

Romans 8:1-3 reads,

1 There is therefore now no condemnation to them which are in Christ Jesus, who walk not after the flesh, but after the Spirit.

[2] For the law of the Spirit of life in Christ Jesus hath made me free from the law of sin and death.

[3] For what the law could not do, in that it was weak through the flesh, God sending his own Son in the likeness of sinful flesh, and for sin, condemned sin in the flesh.

John 14:6 reads,

[6] Jesus saith unto him, I am the way, the truth, and the life: no man cometh unto the Father, but by me.

STEP 7 – PRACTICE THE PRINCIPLES OF JESUS.

When Jesus came into this world, He came teaching and preaching the principles of the Kingdom – a new way of living, a new way of doing things, and the perfect way of overcoming tough times. That is what this book is all about – the principles of Jesus.

Matthew 4:19 reads,

[19] And he saith unto them, Follow me, and I will make you fishers of men.

Matthew 7:24-28 reads,

24 Therefore whosoever heareth these sayings of mine, and doeth them, I will liken him unto a wise man, which built his house upon a rock:

25 And the rain descended, and the floods came, and the winds blew, and beat upon that house; and it fell not: for it was founded upon a rock.

26 And every one that heareth these sayings of mine, and doeth them not, shall be likened unto a foolish man, which built his house upon the sand:

27 And the rain descended, and the floods came, and the winds blew, and beat upon that house; and it fell: and great was the fall of it.

28 And it came to pass, when Jesus had ended these sayings, the people were astonished at his doctrine

Matthew 9:35-39 reads,

35 And Jesus went about all the cities and villages, teaching in their synagogues, and preaching the gospel of the kingdom, and healing every sickness and every disease among the people.

[36] But when he saw the multitudes, he was moved with compassion on them, because they fainted, and were scattered abroad, as sheep having no shepherd.

[37] Then saith he unto his disciples, The harvest truly is plenteous, but the labourers are few;

[38] Pray ye therefore the Lord of the harvest that he will send forth labourers into his harvest.

Acts 10:38 reads,

[38] How God anointed Jesus of Nazareth with the Holy Ghost and with power: who went about doing good, and healing all that were oppressed of the devil; for God was with him.

Matthew 5:1-14 reads,

1 And seeing the multitudes, he went up into a mountain: and when he was set, his disciples came unto him:

[2] And he opened his mouth, and taught them, saying,

[3] Blessed are the poor in spirit: for theirs is the kingdom of heaven.

[4] Blessed are they that mourn: for they shall be comforted.

[5] Blessed are the meek: for they shall inherit the earth.

6 Blessed are they which do hunger and thirst after righteousness: for they shall be filled.

7 Blessed are the merciful: for they shall obtain mercy.

8 Blessed are the pure in heart: for they shall see God.

9 Blessed are the peacemakers: for they shall be called the children of God.

10 Blessed are they which are persecuted for righteousness' sake: for theirs is the kingdom of heaven.

11 Blessed are ye, when men shall revile you, and persecute you, and shall say all manner of evil against you falsely, for my sake.

12 Rejoice, and be exceeding glad: for great is your reward in heaven: for so persecuted they the prophets which were before you.

13 Ye are the salt of the earth: but if the salt have lost his savour, wherewith shall it be salted? it is thenceforth good for nothing, but to be cast out, and to be trodden under foot of men.

14 Ye are the light of the world. A city that is set on an hill cannot be hid.

If you practice this principle, you will never again be Satan's victim. You are an overcomer!

STEP 8 – HAVE PURPOSE FOR LIVING.

Locating and discovering your purpose for living is a vital key to overcoming all tough times. In 1 John 3:8, Jesus knew His purpose; no wonder any tough times could stop Him. When you discover your purpose and begin to pursue and live it, nothing can stop you. No matter how hard the devil tries, a person with purpose is a terror to the devil.

1 John 3:8 reads,

8 He that committeth sin is of the devil; for the devil sinneth from the beginning. For this purpose the Son of God was manifested, that he might destroy the works of the devil.

Jeremiah 29:11 reads,

11 For I know the thoughts that I think toward you, saith the LORD, thoughts of peace, and not of evil, to give you an expected end.

Ephesians 2:10 reads,

[10] For we are his workmanship, created in Christ Jesus unto good works, which God hath before ordained that we should walk in them.

Revelation 4:11 reads,

[11] Thou art worthy, O Lord, to receive glory and honour and power: for thou hast created all things, and for thy pleasure they are and were created.

Matthew 28:18-20 reads,

[18] And Jesus came and spake unto them, saying, All power is given unto me in heaven and in earth.

[19] Go ye therefore, and teach all nations, baptizing them in the name of the Father, and of the Son, and of the Holy Ghost:

[20] Teaching them to observe all things whatsoever I have commanded you: and, lo, I am with you always, even unto the end of the world. Amen.

1 Peter 2:9 reads,

[9] But ye are a chosen generation, a royal priesthood, an holy nation, a peculiar people; that ye should shew

forth the praises of him who hath called you out of darkness into his marvellous light.

STEP 9 – PARTNER WITH OTHERS.

Relationship is the key to life. I submit to you without partnership nothing works. People are suffering today, because they are yet to find out that they were designed by God for partnership. There is no lone ranger in this world. Even Jesus needed disciples to fulfill His mission on earth. Stop suffering alone, locate the godly partners already around you and live. The moment you discover the power of partnership, all tough times and crisis will be eliminated.

Ecclesiastes 4:9-13 reads,

9 Two are better than one; because they have a good reward for their labour.

10 For if they fall, the one will lift up his fellow: but woe to him that is alone when he falleth; for he hath not another to help him up.

11 Again, if two lie together, then they have heat: but how can one be warm alone?

12 And if one prevail against him, two shall withstand him; and a threefold cord is not quickly broken.

13 Better is a poor and a wise child than an old and foolish king, who will no more be admonished.

Genesis 2:18 reads,

18 And the LORD God said, It is not good that the man should be alone; I will make him an help meet for him.

Matthew 18:18-19 reads,

18 Verily I say unto you, Whatsoever ye shall bind on earth shall be bound in heaven: and whatsoever ye shall loose on earth shall be loosed in heaven.

19 Again I say unto you, That if two of you shall agree on earth as touching any thing that they shall ask, it shall be done for them of my Father which is in heaven.

You were designed for relationship, do not fight it, and do not run from it. Embrace partnership and win today.

STEP 10 – PERSIST.

The most powerful virtue of all is the virtue of persistence. People quit at the slightest attack, pain, crisis, or failure, but every winner is persistent. Without persistency there will be no Christianity. Without persistency there will be no life. Jesus went all the way. The Bible is filled with men and women who persisted to the end. You are reading this book today because of persistence. I did not quit even when all hell broke loose. Press on today, and you will be glad you did. Even in tough times; remember tough times come to stop you, but you are an over comer. Never ever give up. Press on to the very end.

Philippians 3:14 reads,

[14] ***I press toward the mark for the prize of the high calling of God in Christ Jesus.***

Matthew 24:12-13 reads,

[12] ***And because iniquity shall abound, the love of many shall wax cold.***

[13] ***But he that shall endure unto the end, the same shall be saved.***

Revelation 2:25-28 reads,

[25] ***But that which ye have already hold fast till I come.***

26 And he that overcometh, and keepeth my works unto the end, to him will I give power over the nations:

27 And he shall rule them with a rod of iron; as the vessels of a potter shall they be broken to shivers: even as I received of my Father.

28 And I will give him the morning star.

Press on today, the victory is already yours. There is a breakthrough waiting for the persistent. You cannot afford to turn back now. God is in you and you cannot fail or lose. Move on in faith and enjoy the victory

STEP 11 – PATIENTLY GO THROUGH THE PROCESS.

Life is all about process. Understanding this will help put the devil to shame. There is nothing in life you can do that will not require a process. When a child is born, he or she must go through the process of growth. When a tree is planted, it goes through the process of dying, resurrection, and then growth. Everything goes through a process. People fret, panic, cry, complain, and quit when they do not know the law of process. Patiently go through the process, knowing that tough times never last but God's people do, forever.

Hebrews 6:12 reads,

12 That ye be not slothful, but followers of them who through faith and patience inherit the promises.

Hebrews 10:35-38 reads,

35 Cast not away therefore your confidence, which hath great recompence of reward.

36 For ye have need of patience, that, after ye have done the will of God, ye might receive the promise.

37 For yet a little while, and he that shall come will come, and will not tarry.

38 Now the just shall live by faith: but if any man draw back, my soul shall have no pleasure in him.

Hebrews 12:1-3 reads,

1 Wherefore seeing we also are compassed about with so great a cloud of witnesses, let us lay aside every weight, and the sin which doth so easily beset us, and let us run with patience the race that is set before us,

2 Looking unto Jesus the author and finisher of our faith; who for the joy that was set before him endured the cross, despising the shame, and is set down at the right hand of the throne of God.

***3 For consider him that endured such contradiction
of sinners against himself, lest ye be wearied and faint
in your minds.***

James 5:4-7 reads,

***4 Behold, the hire of the labourers who have reaped
down your fields, which is of you kept back by fraud,
crieth: and the cries of them which have reaped are
entered into the ears of the Lord of sabaoth.***
***5 Ye have lived in pleasure on the earth, and been
wanton; ye have nourished your hearts, as in a day of
slaughter.***
***6 Ye have condemned and killed the just; and he doth
not resist you.***
***7 Be patient therefore, brethren, unto the coming of
the Lord. Behold, the husbandman waiteth for the precious fruit of the earth, and hath long patience for it,
until he receive the early and latter rain.***

Remember weeping may endure for a night, but joy cometh in the morning. Go through your faith fights confidently knowing that this is just a process and that God is going to show up. Remember tough times never last and that you are an overcomer!

Philippians 1:6 reads,

[6] ***Being confident of this very thing, that he which hath begun a good work in you will perform it until the day of Jesus Christ.***

STEP 12 – PRAISE YOUR WAY OUT.

Praise pleases God; praise is a weapon against the devil. The devil cannot stand praise; he does not understand praise, and he fears praise. You disarm him with praise forever. That is why the Bible says in Psalm 107, "*Oh that men will praise the Lord, for His mercy and for His goodness and wonderful works.*" Praise is your sure way out of tough times.

Psalm 34:1 reads,

I will bless the LORD at all times: his praise shall continually be in my mouth.

Psalm 11:164 reads,

Seven times a day do I praise thee because of thy righteous judgements.

Psalm 65 reads,

1 Praise waiteth for thee, O God, in Sion: and unto thee shall the vow be performed.

2 O thou that hearest prayer, unto thee shall all flesh come.

3 Iniquities prevail against me: as for our transgressions, thou shalt purge them away.

4 Blessed is the man whom thou choosest, and causest to approach unto thee, that he may dwell in thy courts: we shall be satisfied with the goodness of thy house, even of thy holy temple.

5 By terrible things in righteousness wilt thou answer us, O God of our salvation; who art the confidence of all the ends of the earth, and of them that are afar off upon the sea:

6 Which by his strength setteth fast the mountains; being girded with power:

7 Which stilleth the noise of the seas, the noise of their waves, and the tumult of the people.

8 They also that dwell in the uttermost parts are afraid at thy tokens: thou makest the outgoings of the morning and evening to rejoice.

[9] Thou visitest the earth, and waterest it: thou greatly enrichest it with the river of God, which is full of water: thou preparest them corn, when thou hast so provided for it.

[10] Thou waterest the ridges thereof abundantly: thou settlest the furrows thereof: thou makest it soft with showers: thou blessest the springing thereof.

[11] Thou crownest the year with thy goodness; and thy paths drop fatness.

[12] They drop upon the pastures of the wilderness: and the little hills rejoice on every side.

[13] The pastures are clothed with flocks; the valleys also are covered over with corn; they shout for joy, they also sing.

Psalm 150 reads,

1 Praise ye the LORD. Praise God in his sanctuary: praise him in the firmament of his power.

[2] Praise him for his mighty acts: praise him according to his excellent greatness.

[3] Praise him with the sound of the trumpet: praise him with the psaltery and harp.

[4] ***Praise him with the timbrel and dance: praise him with stringed instruments and organs.***

[5] ***Praise him upon the loud cymbals: praise him upon the high sounding cymbals.***

[6] ***Let everything that hath breath praise the LORD. Praise ye the LORD.***

When you praise God, all heaven will break loose upon you and your situation. When you praise God, demons run and Satan bows. It happened for Paul and Silas, Daniel, Jehoshaphat, and it must happen for you. I have personally seen the wonders of praise, and I know it will work for you; if only you work at it and practice it daily all of your life.

Chapter 6

7 SECRETS TO OVERCOMING TOUGH TIMES

As Revealed in Genesis 41:1-37

A secret is an important, special, valuable information, idea or substance kept from general knowledge. It is also something done, made or carried out without the knowledge of others. A secret is something hidden from sight or concealed. It is something precious that is not common.

If everybody has access to the secret of success, then everybody will be successful. Secrets are not common. Ever story has a secret, every successful person or business has a secret that others do not have access to – that is why they are succeeding.

GOD AND SECRETS

The Bible tells us that God is a God of secrets.

1. Joseph. Genesis 41:32-57

In the story above, God gave Pharaoh a dream, but the interpretation was hidden. God gave Joseph the secret to interpret the dream and because of the secrets given to him by God, Joseph excelled, increased, and succeeded. Therefore, you will excel in Jesus' name. Just as God gave Joseph the secrets to overcoming the famine/tough times in Egypt, so is the Lord placing in your hands right now the awe inspiring secrets for a turnaround for you – the seven secrets that will bring you out of all tough times, crisis, difficulty, problems, or storms of life. Get ready to come out today.

As you are reading this book, meditate and study it deeply. You will never be the same again in your life. Your tough times are vanishing right now, you will see them again no more. Remember, tough time never last.

The fact that you have read this book this far proves you are serious and hungry for a major move of God in your own life. Remember, Jesus is the same yesterday, today, and forever.

Let us look at a couple of scriptures that prove God is a God of secrets, to prepare you for what lies ahead of you. These secrets work. Today, I am who I am because of these amazing secrets of God.

2. Job

Job 29:4 reads,

4 As I was in the days of my youth, when the secret of God was upon my tabernacle.

Job 15:8 reads,

8 Hast thou heard the secret of God? and dost thou restrain wisdom to thyself?

Job understood the power of the secrets of God hence his success and breakthrough in life. He talked about it and referred to it in his prayer.

3. **David**

Psalm 25:14 reads,

14 The secret of the LORD is with them that fear him; and he will shew them his covenant.

Psalm 27:5-6 reads,

5 For in the time of trouble he shall hide me in his pavilion: in the secret of his tabernacle shall he hide me; he shall set me up upon a rock.

6 And now shall mine head be lifted up above mine enemies round about me: therefore will I offer in his tabernacle sacrifices of joy; I will sing, yea, I will sing praises unto the Lord.

Psalm 91:1-3 reads,

1 He that dwelleth in the secret place of the most High shall abide under the shadow of the Almighty.

[2] I will say of the LORD, He is my refuge and my fortress: my God; in him will I trust.

[3] Surely he shall deliver thee from the snare of the fowler, and from the noisome pestilence.

Psalm 31:20 reads,

[20] Thou shalt hide them in the secret of thy presence from the pride of man: thou shalt keep them secretly in a pavilion from the strife of tongues.

Psalm 139:14-18 reads,

[14] I will praise thee; for I am fearfully and wonderfully made: marvelous are thy works; and that my soul knoweth right well.

15 My substance was not hid from thee, when I was made in secret, and curiously wrought in the lowest parts of the earth.

16 Thine eyes did see my substance, yet being unperfect; and in thy book all my members were written, which in continuance were fashioned, when as yet there was none of them.

17 How precious also are thy thoughts unto me, O God! how great is the sum of them!

18 If I should count them, they are more in number than the sand: when I awake, I am still with thee.

David enjoyed the presence of God because he had secrets others did not have access to. He became a man after the heart of God because he knew the secrets to God's heart and did them. You can practice and live by the principles

4. Daniel

Daniel is another man that enjoyed the secrets of God. He had a personal relationship and an encounter with God that many people are yet to understand and enjoy. He knew secrets from God.

Daniel 2:22 reads,

22 He revealeth the deep and secret things: he knoweth what is in the darkness, and the light dwelleth with him.

Daniel 2:28 reads,

28 But there is a God in heaven that revealeth secrets, and maketh known to the king Nebuchadnezzar what shall be in the latter days. Thy dream, and the visions of thy head upon thy bed, are these.

Daniel 4:9 reads,

9 O Belteshazzar, master of the magicians, because I know that the spirit of the holy gods is in thee, and no secret troubleth thee, tell me the visions of my dream that I have seen, and the interpretation thereof.

Daniel was not ordinary, he was operating in a level where everybody marveled and wondered; even the king submitted to Daniel when he saw the display of God's secrets and power. The entire nation submitted to the God of Daniel, and he changed history because of secrets.

Daniel 2:47 reads,

47 The king answered unto Daniel, and said, Of a truth it is, that your God is a God of gods, and a Lord of kings, and a revealer of secrets, seeing thou couldest reveal this secret.

Like Daniel, get ready to overcome all the tough times in your life. You are coming out of every tough time in Jesus' name. Remember, this too shall pass and joy cometh in the morning.

5. Amos

Another person that understood secrets was Amos, the prophet. Amos made a powerful statement and gave us a wonderful revelation about the God of secrets; as you will see from the scripture, we are just about to read below.

Amos 3:7 reads,

Surely, the Lord GOD will do nothing but he revealeth his secret unto his servants the prophets.

God will never do anything on earth without revealing the secrets to His servants the prophets. Can you imagine that? God will do nothing without revealing the secret to someone first.

How many secrets has God been trying to reveal to you that you have ignored or failed to adhere to; either due to you ignorance or carelessness and you are now suffering the consequences? That is why this book, apart from the Bible, is the most powerful tool in your life today, to guide you and direct you the rest of the days of your life on earth. You will never lose in life or be defeated again. It will help empower you for the future. When you receive God's secrets and apply them like all the people in the stories we have read, you will be numbered among them and enjoy the very best of God; and be a blessing to your generation.

Deuteronomy 29:29 reads,

[29] The secret things belong unto the LORD our God: but those things which are revealed belong unto us and to our children forever, that we may do all the words of this law.

Look at the scripture again, there is so much power in it – "the secret things that are revealed belong to us." When God reveals anything, He reveals to redeem, He reveals to release, He reveals to restore, and He reveals to raise up. With this revelation in your hand, God will take you to a greater height in life and ministry.

When Joseph took delivery of the secrets in his own generation, he rose to the highest position in the nation of Egypt. He became a force to be respected and worked with. That same anointing is coming on you now as you are reading and studying this book.

Take a moment and meditate on these words, you will never be the same again. This is a new day for you and your release is here.

JESUS TAUGHT ABOUT SECRETS

Jesus also taught and confirmed the God is a God of secrets; this is like the icing on the cake. Whatever Jesus says is final, He is the Lord of lords.

Matthew 4:4-6 reads,

4 But he answered and said, It is written, Man shall not live by bread alone, but by every word that proceedeth out of the mouth of God.

5 Then the devil taketh him up into the holy city, and setteth him on a pinnacle of the temple,

6 And saith unto him, If thou be the Son of God, cast thyself down: for it is written, He shall give his angels charge concerning thee: and in their hands they shall bear thee up, lest at any time thou dash thy foot against a stone.

Matthew 6:18 reads,

[18] That thou appear not unto men to fast, but unto thy Father which is in secret: and thy Father, which seeth in secret, shall reward thee openly.

John 15:15 reads,

[15] Henceforth I call you not servants; for the servant knoweth not what his lord doeth: but I have called you friends; for all things that I have heard of my Father I have made known unto you.

Jesus was the best kept secret, but now He is made manifest. When He came, He revealed all the hidden plans and secrets of God. He was the best kept secret.

6. Paul

Paul, the great apostle, was used mightily of God. He wrote more than half of the New Testament. He enjoyed the secrets of God more than the twelve apostles put together. He did all the exploits because of secrets. He downloaded secrets from the throne room of the Most High. You will enjoy the same grace in the name of Jesus Christ.

1 Corinthians 2:7-12 reads,

7 But we speak the wisdom of God in a mystery, even the hidden wisdom, which God ordained before the world unto our glory:

8 Which none of the princes of this world knew: for had they known it, they would not have crucified the Lord of glory.

9 But as it is written, Eye hath not seen, nor ear heard, neither have entered into the heart of man, the things which God hath prepared for them that love him.

10 But God hath revealed them unto us by his Spirit: for the Spirit searcheth all things, yea, the deep things of God.

11 For what man knoweth the things of a man, save the spirit of man which is in him? even so the things of God knoweth no man, but the Spirit of God.

12 Now we have received, not the spirit of the world, but the spirit which is of God; that we might know the things that are freely given to us of God.

Ephesians 3:9-12 reads,

9 And to make all men see what is the fellowship of the mystery, which from the beginning of the world hath been hid in God, who created all things by Jesus Christ:

[10] To the intent that now unto the principalities and powers in heavenly places might be known by the church the manifold wisdom of God,

[11] According to the eternal purpose which he purposed in Christ Jesus our Lord:

[12] In whom we have boldness and access with confidence by the faith of him.

Colossians 1:26-29 reads,

[26] Even the mystery which hath been hid from ages and from generations, but now is made manifest to his saints:

[27] To whom God would make known what is the riches of the glory of this mystery among the Gentiles; which is Christ in you, the hope of glory:

[28] Whom we preach, warning every man, and teaching every man in all wisdom; that we may present every man perfect in Christ Jesus:

[29] Whereunto I also labour, striving according to his working, which worketh in me mightily.

Paul knew what others did not know; that was the source of his strength and the secret of all his exploits. We are still studying and enjoying the secrets that Paul downloaded from heaven. May you be blessed and changed by the secrets in this book and become a blessing to your generations.

7 SECRETS TO OVERCOMING TOUGH TIMES

These are the 7 Secrets to overcoming your tough times. Apply them and you will never ever be defeated another day in your life. You are not going to take "no" for an answer. Your day is here. Receive them, follow the order, and begin to enjoy what Joseph enjoyed.

Secret #1 – Wisdom

No Wisdom, No Winning

No Wisdom, No Wealth

Secret #2–Planning

No Planning, No Productivity

No Planning, No Prevailing

Secret #3 – Partnership

No Partnership, No Promotion

No Partnership, No Profit

Secret #4–Faith

No Faith, No Future

No Faith, No Finance

Secret #5 – Change

No Change, No Chance

No Change, No Creativity

Secret #6 – Obedience

No Obedience, No Open Doors

No Obedience, No Open Heavens

Secret #7 – Problem Solver

No Service, No Success

Solve Problems and Succeed Forever

Chapter 7

SECRET #1 WISDOM

Genesis 41:33 reads,

> [33] ***Now therefore let Pharaoh look out a man discreet and wise, and set him over the land of Egypt.***

Proverbs 4:5-7 reads,

> [5] ***Get wisdom, get understanding: forget it not; neither decline from the words of my mouth.***
>
> [6] ***Forsake her not, and she shall preserve thee: love her, and she shall keep thee.***

[7] Wisdom is the principal thing; therefore get wisdom: and with all thy getting get understanding.

With the deadly tough times facing the world today, your sure way out is the way of wisdom. This wisdom is not man's wisdom for that has failed, nor the world's wisdom for that has collapsed. Everything man has known has completely failed. Only the wisdom of God will bring you out. God told Joseph, for Egypt to overcome the global crisis they were in and to survive the tough times, they needed wisdom. For you to come out of any kind of tough time, you need wisdom.

Proverbs 16:16 reads,

[16] How much better is it to get wisdom than gold! and to get understanding rather to be chosen than silver!

Proverbs 8:11-25 reads,

[11] For wisdom is better than rubies; and all the things that may be desired are not to be compared to it.

[12] I wisdom dwell with prudence, and find out knowledge of witty inventions.

13 The fear of the LORD is to hate evil: pride, and arrogance, and the evil way, and the froward mouth, do I hate.

14 Counsel is mine, and sound wisdom: I am understanding; I have strength.

15 By me kings reign, and princes decree justice.

16 By me princes rule, and nobles, even all the judges of the earth.

17 I love them that love me; and those that seek me early shall find me.

18 Riches and honour are with me; yea, durable riches and righteousness.

19 My fruit is better than gold, yea, than fine gold; and my revenue than choice silver.

20 I lead in the way of righteousness, in the midst of the paths of judgment:

21 That I may cause those that love me to inherit substance; and I will fill their treasures.

22 The LORD possessed me in the beginning of his way, before his works of old.

23 I was set up from everlasting, from the beginning, or ever the earth was.

[24] When there were no depths, I was brought forth; when there were no fountains abounding with water.

[25] Before the mountains were settled, before the hills was I brought forth.

Proverbs 24:3-7 reads,

[3] Through wisdom is an house builded; and by understanding it is established:

[4] And by knowledge shall the chambers be filled with all precious and pleasant riches.

[5] A wise man is strong; yea, a man of knowledge increaseth strength.

[6] For by wise counsel thou shalt make thy war: and in multitude of counsellors there is safety.

[7] Wisdom is too high for a fool: he openeth not his mouth in the gate.

The scriptures clearly tell us that through wisdom is a house built, which means you cannot build without wisdom. It also means with wisdom you can build from ground zero again, no matter how bad the situation is. The Word of God says you can build back again with wisdom.

1 Corinthians 2:6-14 reads,

[6] Howbeit we speak wisdom among them that are perfect: yet not the wisdom of this world, nor of the princes of this world, that come to nought:

[7] But we speak the wisdom of God in a mystery, even the hidden wisdom, which God ordained before the world unto our glory:

[8] Which none of the princes of this world knew: for had they known it, they would not have crucified the Lord of glory.

[9] But as it is written, Eye hath not seen, nor ear heard, neither have entered into the heart of man, the things which God hath prepared for them that love him.

[10] But God hath revealed them unto us by his Spirit: for the Spirit searcheth all things, yea, the deep things of God.

[11] For what man knoweth the things of a man, save the spirit of man which is in him? even so the things of God knoweth no man, but the Spirit of God.

[12] Now we have received, not the spirit of the world, but the spirit which is of God; that we might know the things that are freely given to us of God.

[13] ***Which things also we speak, not in the words which man's wisdom teacheth, but which the Holy Ghost teacheth; comparing spiritual things with spiritual.***

[14] ***But the natural man receiveth not the things of the Spirit of God: for they are foolishness unto him: neither can he know them, because they are spiritually discerned.***

GODLY WISDOM

The way to overcome your tough times is to apply godly wisdom. Godly wisdom is God Himself; embrace that wisdom and all hell will bow to you.

HOW TO APPLY GODLY WISDOM IN TOUGH TIMES

12 WAYS TO EXERCISE WISDOM

1. INVITE GOD

Invite God into your situation, no matter how bad it is. Remember, with God all things are possible. When you get God involved, the case is over. God is enough.

2. INFORMATION

Go for information, especially on the issues you are facing. Knowledge is power. What you do not know can kill you.

3. INSTRUCTIONS

Proverbs 4:13

Take fast hold of instruction; let her not go: keep her; for she is thy life.

Instruction according to the Bible is your life. When you follow instructions, you will increase.

4. INTIMACY

Get into an intimate relationship with God and with people who are more successful and smarter than you.

Proverbs 13:20 reads,

He that walketh with wise men shall be wise: but a companion of fools shall be destroyed.

5. INTEGRITY

You will need integrity to win and succeed in life. How is your integrity? Integrity is everything. No integrity, no increase. People and God cannot believe you without integrity.

6. IMAGINATION

God gave you and me the gift of imagination, but unfortunately many do not use theirs. In tough times, people only imagine the worst instead of the best. Begin to use your imagination in the right way.

Genesis 11:6 reads,

And the LORD said, Behold, the people is one, and they have all one language; and this they begin to do: and now nothing will be restrained from them, which they have imagined to do.

7. INVESTMENT

To overcome tough times, you have to check your manner of investments. How are your investments? By investment, I mean your time, energy, and money should all to be channeled in the right direction.

8. IDEAS

In all tough times you will go through, the Lord will always present you with fresh ideas on what to do.

Remember, ideas rule the world. No ideas, No influence. Go for every idea God gives you, do not trash it; it will see you through, because it is of God.

9. INVOLVE OTHERS

Life was never meant to be lived alone, you cannot do all the fighting alone. Therefore, you must involve others. With the global economic crisis, major companies are merging for greater productivity. Involve others in your life, dream, vision, battle, and future. Remember, a tree cannot make a forest and the Bible says two are better than one.

Ecclesiastes 4:9 reads,

Two are better than one; because they have a good reward for their labor.

10. IMPLEMENTATION

This is where the rubber meets the road. To acquire all this information without implementation is deadly. I have seen over the years that people will buy books and materials without implementing what they have learned. In all tough times, you must implement what you have learned; that is the only way out – that is wisdom.

11. IMPROVEMENT

There is always a way you can improve yourself. You have got to keep on improving in every way you can. Do not even give up; it is never too late to improve. You must improve in all areas of your life – spiritually, physically, mentally, martially, and financially. Improve today.

12. INCREASE

Psalm 115:14 reads,

The LORD shall increase you more and more, you and your children.

The Bible declares God will increase you more and more. God is a God of increase. You must know that life is about increase. No matter how tough the situation is, the Lord will use it to increase you. Go for increase today. Increase is your portion in tough times. You must increase in five areas.

- **Wisdom** – Increase in wisdom
- **Seed** – Increase in seed sowing
- **Search** – Increase your search for wisdom
- **Hunger** – Increase in your hunger for God.
- **Goal** – Increase in your goals for greatness

SECRET #1 TO OVERCOMING TOUGH TIMES IS WISDOM

Ecclesiastes 7:12

For wisdom is defence, and money is a defence:
But the excellency of knowledge is,
That wisdom giveth life to them that have it.

Ecclesiastes 7:19

Wisdom stengtheneth the wise more
Than ten mighty men which are in the city.
Embrace wisdom and win today.

PLAN NEVER TO GIVE UP.
PLAN VICTORY AND NOT DEFEAT.PLAN TO WIN AND NOT TO FAIL.
GOD HAS A PLAN FOR YOU, EMBRACE IT.

Chapter 8

SECRET #2
PLANNING

God is a planner and I believe that all of His children and anyone connected to Him must become a planner.

Planning is the way out of all tough times. As I travel around the world, I have noticed that a major problem people have is they all talk about their problems, cry about them, fret and worry, but never plan their way out. Everywhere you turn, you hear of problems and about doom and gloom, but nobody is offering a plan of action to get out of the predicament.

That is why God is releasing into your hands this powerful tool to help guide you on exactly what to do and how to do it with examples of those who practiced the secrets and how they overcame. This is a life time resource that will bless you over and over again. When God gave Joseph the secrets for Egypt, he told them to plan their way out. Remember the saying, "Failure to plan is planning to fail."

The Lord showed me this quote one day, "Powerful Preparation Prevents Poor Performance. Egypt was told to plan ahead, prepare ahead, and pray ahead in order to overcome tough times.

Genesis 41:34-36 reads,

[34] ***Let Pharaoh do this, and let him appoint officers over the land, and take up the fifth part of the land of Egypt in the seven plenteous years.***

[35] ***And let them gather all the food of those good years that come, and lay up corn under the hand of Pharaoh, and let them keep food in the cities.***

[36] ***And that food shall be for store to the land against the seven years of famine, which shall be in the land of Egypt; that the land perish not through the famine.***

The secret of planning is that many do not value the power and preciousness of planning. When you embrace planning, you defeat tough times forever.

Luke 14:28-38 reads,

28 For which of you, intending to build a tower, sitteth
not down first, and counteth the cost, whether he have
sufficient to finish it?
29 Lest haply, after he hath laid the foundation, and is
not able to finish it, all that behold it begin to mock him,
30 Saying, This man began to build, and was not able
to finish.
31 Or what king, going to make war against another
king, sitteth not down first, and consulteth whether he
be able with ten thousand to meet him that cometh
against him with twenty thousand?
32 Or else, while the other is yet a great way off, he
sendeth an ambassage, and desireth conditions of peace.
33 So likewise, whosoever he be of you that forsaketh
not all that he hath, he cannot be my disciple.
34 Salt is good: but if the salt have lost his savour,
wherewith shall it be seasoned?
35 It is neither fit for the land, nor yet for the dung-
hill; but men cast it out. He that hath ears to hear, let
him hear.

Jesus taught and practiced planning all throughout His ministry. From Matthew to John, the gospels prove and show to us that Jesus was a planner. No wonder He accomplished more than anybody in this world, and He did it all in 33 ½ years. God has planned heaven and hell. Jesus said in John 14:1-3, "I go to prepare a place for you." Remember, no planning, no prosperity. Start planning today. Mike Murdock will always say, "If you cannot plan a day, how will you plan a week, a month, a year or your life?" Your planning is the key to overcoming tough times.

AREAS OF PLANNING

- Plan your day.
- Plan your week.
- Plan your month.
- Plan your year.
- Plan your health.
- Plan your wealth.
- Plan your purpose in life.
- Plan your family.
- Plan your finance.
- Plan your time.
- Plan your relationship with God and man.
- Plan your way to the top.
- Plan your way of escape.

- Plan your giving.
- Plan your future.

Plan never to give up, plan victory and not defeat. Plan to win and not to fail. God has a plan for you, embrace it.

Jeremiah 29:11-12 reads,

11 For I know the thoughts that I think toward you, saith the LORD, thoughts of peace, and not of evil, to give you an expected end.

12 Then shall ye call upon me, and ye shall go and pray unto me, and I will hearken unto you.

ALWAYS HAVE AN EXIT PLAN!

PRACTICE IT DAILY.

IT'S NOT TOO LATE TO MAKE A PLAN.

Chapter 9

SECRET #3
PARTNERSHIP AND NETWORKING

God has been a God of partnership and networking from the very beginning of the world. The Lord has used the principle of partnership up through today. He does nothing without partnership. So must you.

The reason for failure and difficulty in the lives of people is a lack of knowledge and understanding of the power of partnership. Partnership is not just a suggestion; it is the way of life. Relationship is the key to life. You will never achieve anything worthwhile or significant without partnership. It is a secret that will put you on top. That is the reason the devil attacks relationship more than anything. Check out on all your tough times and you will trace it to bad and toxic relationships.

God told Joseph that Egypt will overcome their tough times, but only if they partner with others – getting people involved in the battle and warfare of tough times.

Genesis 41:37-38 reads,

37 And the thing was good in the eyes of Pharaoh, and in the eyes of all his servants.

38 And Pharaoh said unto his servants, Can we find such a one as this is, a man in whom the Spirit of God is?

Even Pharaoh knew that the way out and forward is to partner with the God of Israel and partner with Joseph, the man with the secrets; a man smarter than him and his magicians. They would have suffered for life if they had never partnered. No one can fight and overcome these tough times alone. Partner with the right people now.

REMEMBER, NO PARTNERSHIP, NO PROBLEM SOLUTION

Ecclesiastes 4:9 reads,

9 Two are better than one; because they have a good reward for their labour.

NO PARTNERSHIP, NO PROFIT

Genesis 2:18 reads,

[18] ***And the LORD God said, It is not good that the man should be alone; I will make him an help meet for him.***

Another word for partnership is teamwork, teaming up with stronger people than you. Teaming up with wiser people than you will eventually help you overcome tough times.

Proverbs 13:20 reads,

He that walketh with wise men shall be wise: but a companion of fools shall be destroyed.

When God wants to do anything, He looks for someone to partner with. If God cannot do anything without partnership, how do you think you will overcome? Partnership is the secret to all successes.

FIVE MAJOR PEOPLE GOD PARTNERED WITH IN THE BIBLE

The Bible is clear on the power of partnership. With that in mind, let us take a look at five major people in the Bible God partnered with.

- Adam and Eve

- Noah
- Abraham
- Moses
- Mary (Jesus' mother)

1. ADAM AND EVE

They were the first whom God partnered with for the benefit of all people on the earth, but they lost it. Let us read two scriptures in the book of Genesis.

Genesis 1:26-31 reads,

26 And God said, Let us make man in our image, after our likeness: and let them have dominion over the fish of the sea, and over the fowl of the air, and over the cattle, and over all the earth, and over every creeping thing that creepeth upon the earth.

27 So God created man in his own image, in the image of God created he him; male and female created he them.

28 And God blessed them, and God said unto them, Be fruitful, and multiply, and replenish the earth, and subdue it: and have dominion over the fish of the sea, and over the fowl of the air, and over every living thing that moveth upon the earth.

[29] And God said, Behold, I have given you every herb bearing seed, which is upon the face of all the earth, and every tree, in the which is the fruit of a tree yielding seed; to you it shall be for meat.

[30] And to every beast of the earth, and to every fowl of the air, and to everything that creepeth upon the earth, wherein there is life, I have given every green herb for meat: and it was so.

[31] And God saw everything that he had made, and, behold, it was very good. And the evening and the morning were the sixth day.

Genesis 2:18-25 reads,

[18] And the LORD God said, It is not good that the man should be alone; I will make him an help meet for him.

[19] And out of the ground the LORD God formed every beast of the field, and every fowl of the air; and brought them unto Adam to see what he would call them: and whatsoever Adam called every living creature, that was the name thereof.

[20] And Adam gave names to all cattle, and to the fowl of the air, and to every beast of the field; but for Adam there was not found an help meet for him.

21 And the LORD God caused a deep sleep to fall upon Adam, and he slept: and he took one of his ribs, and closed up the flesh instead thereof;

22 And the rib, which the LORD God had taken from man, made he a woman, and brought her unto the man.

23 And Adam said, This is now bone of my bones, and flesh of my flesh: she shall be called Woman, because she was taken out of Man.

24 Therefore shall a man leave his father and his mother, and shall cleave unto his wife: and they shall be one flesh.

25 And they were both naked, the man and his wife, and were not ashamed.

When you miss it in partnership, your tough times maybe longer than imagined. Just like Adam, his tough times came when he broke his partnership with his Maker and Lover. Connect with the right people today and overcome your tough times.

2. NOAH

God partnered with Noah for the salvation of mankind from the wrath of God and tough times.

Genesis 6:1-22 tells us about this partnership.

1 And it came to pass, when men began to multiply on the face of the earth, and daughters were born unto them,

2 That the sons of God saw the daughters of men that they were fair; and they took them wives of all which they chose.

3 And the LORD said, My spirit shall not always strive with man, for that he also is flesh: yet his days shall be an hundred and twenty years.

4 There were giants in the earth in those days; and also after that, when the sons of God came in unto the daughters of men, and they bare children to them, the same became mighty men which were of old, men of renown.

5 And God saw that the wickedness of man was great in the earth, and that every imagination of the thoughts of his heart was only evil continually.

6 And it repented the LORD that he had made man on the earth, and it grieved him at his heart.

7 And the LORD said, I will destroy man whom I have created from the face of the earth; both man, and beast, and the creeping thing, and the fowls of the air; for it repenteth me that I have made them.

[8] But Noah found grace in the eyes of the LORD.

[9] These are the generations of Noah: Noah was a just man and perfect in his generations, and Noah walked with God.

[10] And Noah begat three sons, Shem, Ham, and Japheth.

[11] The earth also was corrupt before God, and the earth was filled with violence.

[12] And God looked upon the earth, and, behold, it was corrupt; for all flesh had corrupted his way upon the earth.

[13] And God said unto Noah, The end of all flesh is come before me; for the earth is filled with violence through them; and, behold, I will destroy them with the earth.

[14] Make thee an ark of gopher wood; rooms shalt thou make in the ark, and shalt pitch it within and without with pitch.

[15] And this is the fashion which thou shalt make it of: The length of the ark shall be three hundred cubits, the breadth of it fifty cubits, and the height of it thirty cubits.

[16] A window shalt thou make to the ark, and in a cubit shalt thou finish it above; and the door of the ark shalt

thou set in the side thereof; with lower, second, and third stories shalt thou make it.

[17] And, behold, I, even I, do bring a flood of waters upon the earth, to destroy all flesh, wherein is the breath of life, from under heaven; and everything that is in the earth shall die.

[18] But with thee will I establish my covenant; and thou shalt come into the ark, thou, and thy sons, and thy wife, and thy sons' wives with thee.

[19] And of every living thing of all flesh, two of every sort shalt thou bring into the ark, to keep them alive with thee; they shall be male and female.

[20] Of fowls after their kind, and of cattle after their kind, of every creeping thing of the earth after his kind, two of every sort shall come unto thee, to keep them alive.

[21] And take thou unto thee of all food that is eaten, and thou shalt gather it to thee; and it shall be for food for thee, and for them.

[22] Thus did Noah; according to all that God commanded him, so did he.

God saw the righteousness of Noah and partnered with him and his family. As a result they overcame the tough times.

3. ABRAHAM

God partnered with Abraham for a fresh generation of people and to release His blessings upon mankind again. Abraham became the hero of faith when he believed God and partnered with God. Abraham and his generation overcame their tough times.

Genesis 12:1-10 reads,

1 Now the LORD had said unto Abram, Get thee out of
thy country, and from thy kindred, and from thy father's
house, unto a land that I will shew thee:

2 And I will make of thee a great nation, and I will
bless thee, and make thy name great; and thou shalt be
a blessing:

3 And I will bless them that bless thee, and curse him
that curseth thee: and in thee shall all families of the
earth be blessed.

4 So Abram departed, as the LORD had spoken unto
him; and Lot went with him: and Abram was seventy and
five years old when he departed out of Haran.

5 And Abram took Sarai his wife, and Lot his brother's
son, and all their substance that they had gathered, and
the souls that they had gotten in Haran; and they went

forth to go into the land of Canaan; and into the land of Canaan they came.

[6] And Abram passed through the land unto the place of Sichem, unto the plain of Moreh. And the Canaanite was then in the land.

[7] And the LORD appeared unto Abram, and said, Unto thy seed will I give this land: and there builded he an altar unto the LORD, who appeared unto him.

[8] And he removed from thence unto a mountain on the east of Bethel, and pitched his tent, having Bethel on the west, and Hai on the east: and there he builded an altar unto the LORD, and called upon the name of the LORD.

[9] And Abram journeyed, going on still toward the south.

[10] And there was a famine in the land: and Abram went down into Egypt to sojourn there; for the famine was grievous in the land.

Genesis 15:1-16 reads,

1 After these things the word of the LORD came unto Abram in a vision, saying, Fear not, Abram: I am thy shield, and thy exceeding great reward.

[2] And Abram said, LORD God, what wilt thou give me, seeing I go childless, and the steward of my house is this Eliezer of Damascus?

[3] And Abram said, Behold, to me thou hast given no seed: and, lo, one born in my house is mine heir.

[4] And, behold, the word of the LORD came unto him, saying, This shall not be thine heir; but he that shall come forth out of thine own bowels shall be thine heir.

[5] And he brought him forth abroad, and said, Look now toward heaven, and tell the stars, if thou be able to number them: and he said unto him, So shall thy seed be.

[6] And he believed in the LORD; and he counted it to him for righteousness.

[7] And he said unto him, I am the LORD that brought thee out of Ur of the Chaldees, to give thee this land to inherit it.

[8] And he said, LORD God, whereby shall I know that I shall inherit it?

[9] And he said unto him, Take me an heifer of three years old, and a she goat of three years old, and a ram of three years old, and a turtledove, and a young pigeon.

10 And he took unto him all these, and divided them in the midst, and laid each piece one against another: but the birds divided he not.

11 And when the fowls came down upon the carcases, Abram drove them away.

12 And when the sun was going down, a deep sleep fell upon Abram; and, lo, an horror of great darkness fell upon him.

13 And he said unto Abram, Know of a surety that thy seed shall be a stranger in a land that is not theirs, and shall serve them; and they shall afflict them four hundred years;

14 And also that nation, whom they shall serve, will I judge: and afterward shall they come out with great substance.

15 And thou shalt go to thy fathers in peace; thou shalt be buried in a good old age.

16 But in the fourth generation they shall come hither again: for the iniquity of the Amorites is not yet full.

The Bible says the Abraham believed God and partnered with God for his blessing to come on all the earth. When you partner with others, you will overcome tough times.

4. MOSES

Moses was another prophet that God partnered with for the salvation and deliverance of the Israelites from Egypt, and He brought them out. They overcame Egypt and Pharaoh; so will you conquer.

Exodus 3:1-22 reads,

1 Now Moses kept the flock of Jethro his father in law, the priest of Midian: and he led the flock to the backside of the desert, and came to the mountain of God, even to Horeb.

2 And the angel of the LORD appeared unto him in a flame of fire out of the midst of a bush: and he looked, and, behold, the bush burned with fire, and the bush was not consumed.

3 And Moses said, I will now turn aside, and see this great sight, why the bush is not burnt.

4 And when the LORD saw that he turned aside to see, God called unto him out of the midst of the bush, and said, Moses, Moses. And he said, Here am I.

5 And he said, Draw not nigh hither: put off thy shoes from off thy feet, for the place whereon thou standest is holy ground.

6 Moreover he said, I am the God of thy father, the God of Abraham, the God of Isaac, and the God of Jacob. And Moses hid his face; for he was afraid to look upon God.

7 And the LORD said, I have surely seen the affliction of my people which are in Egypt, and have heard their cry by reason of their taskmasters; for I know their sorrows;

8 And I am come down to deliver them out of the hand of the Egyptians, and to bring them up out of that land unto a good land and a large, unto a land flowing with milk and honey; unto the place of the Canaanites, and the Hittites, and the Amorites, and the Perizzites, and the Hivites, and the Jebusites.

9 Now therefore, behold, the cry of the children of Israel is come unto me: and I have also seen the oppression wherewith the Egyptians oppress them.

10 Come now therefore, and I will send thee unto Pharaoh, that thou mayest bring forth my people the children of Israel out of Egypt.

11 And Moses said unto God, Who am I, that I should go unto Pharaoh, and that I should bring forth the children of Israel out of Egypt?

12 And he said, Certainly I will be with thee; and this shall be a token unto thee, that I have sent thee: When

thou hast brought forth the people out of Egypt, ye shall serve God upon this mountain.

13 And Moses said unto God, Behold, when I come unto the children of Israel, and shall say unto them, The God of your fathers hath sent me unto you; and they shall say to me, What is his name? what shall I say unto them?

14 And God said unto Moses, I AM THAT I AM: and he said, Thus shalt thou say unto the children of Israel, I AM hath sent me unto you.

15 And God said moreover unto Moses, Thus shalt thou say unto the children of Israel, the LORD God of your fathers, the God of Abraham, the God of Isaac, and the God of Jacob, hath sent me unto you: this is my name forever, and this is my memorial unto all generations.

16 Go, and gather the elders of Israel together, and say unto them, The LORD God of your fathers, the God of Abraham, of Isaac, and of Jacob, appeared unto me, saying, I have surely visited you, and seen that which is done to you in Egypt:

17 And I have said, I will bring you up out of the affliction of Egypt unto the land of the Canaanites, and the Hittites, and the Amorites, and the Perizzites, and the

Hivites, and the Jebusites, unto a land flowing with milk and honey.

18 And they shall hearken to thy voice: and thou shalt come, thou and the elders of Israel, unto the king of Egypt, and ye shall say unto him, The LORD God of the Hebrews hath met with us: and now let us go, we beseech thee, three days' journey into the wilderness, that we may sacrifice to the LORD our God.

19 And I am sure that the king of Egypt will not let you go, no, not by a mighty hand.

20 And I will stretch out my hand, and smite Egypt with all my wonders which I will do in the midst thereof: and after that he will let you go.

21 And I will give this people favour in the sight of the Egyptians: and it shall come to pass, that, when ye go, ye shall not go empty.

22 But every woman shall borrow of her neighbour, and of her that sojourneth in her house, jewels of silver, and jewels of gold, and raiment: and ye shall put them upon your sons, and upon your daughters; and ye shall spoil the Egyptians.

Moses did exactly as the Lord commanded, and they overcame the Egyptians and their tough times. Expect victory as you partner today in every area of life.

5. MARY (THE MOTHER OF JESUS)

The one major partnership in the New Testament is with Mary, the mother of Jesus. God needed to save you and me from the tough times of hell, sickness, struggle, suffering, sin, and lack, but that was only possible because Mary agreed to partner with God. The world is saved today because someone saw the need to do the unthinkable and today the rest is history. Consequently, you shall make history that can never be forgotten.

Luke 1:26-56 reads,

26 And in the sixth month the angel Gabriel was sent from God unto a city of Galilee, named Nazareth,

27 To a virgin espoused to a man whose name was Joseph, of the house of David; and the virgin's name was Mary.

28 And the angel came in unto her, and said, Hail, thou that art highly favoured, the Lord is with thee: blessed art thou among women.

[29] ***And when she saw him, she was troubled at his saying, and cast in her mind what manner of salutation this should be.***

[30] ***And the angel said unto her, Fear not, Mary: for thou hast found favour with God.***

[31] ***And, behold, thou shalt conceive in thy womb, and bring forth a son, and shalt call his name JESUS.***

[32] ***He shall be great, and shall be called the Son of the Highest: and the Lord God shall give unto him the throne of his father David:***

[33] ***And he shall reign over the house of Jacob forever; and of his kingdom there shall be no end.***

[34] ***Then said Mary unto the angel, How shall this be, seeing I know not a man?***

[35] ***And the angel answered and said unto her, The Holy Ghost shall come upon thee, and the power of the Highest shall overshadow thee: therefore also that holy thing which shall be born of thee shall be called the Son of God.***

[36] ***And, behold, thy cousin Elisabeth, she hath also conceived a son in her old age: and this is the sixth month with her, who was called barren.***

[37] ***For with God nothing shall be impossible.***

*38 And Mary said, Behold the handmaid of the Lord;
be it unto me according to thy word. And the angel
departed from her.*

*39 And Mary arose in those days, and went into the
hill country with haste, into a city of Juda;*

*40 And entered into the house of Zacharias, and
saluted Elisabeth.*

*41 And it came to pass, that, when Elisabeth heard the
salutation of Mary, the babe leaped in her womb; and
Elisabeth was filled with the Holy Ghost:*

*42 And she spake out with a loud voice, and said,
Blessed art thou among women, and blessed is the fruit
of thy womb.*

*43 And whence is this to me, that the mother of my
Lord should come to me?*

*44 For, lo, as soon as the voice of thy salutation sounded
in mine ears, the babe leaped in my womb for joy.*

*45 And blessed is she that believed: for there shall be
a performance of those things which were told her from
the Lord.*

46 And Mary said, My soul doth magnify the Lord,

47 And my spirit hath rejoiced in God my Savior.

***48** For he hath regarded the low estate of his handmaiden: for, behold, from henceforth all generations shall call me blessed.*

***49** For he that is mighty hath done to me great things; and holy is his name.*

***50** And his mercy is on them that fear him from generation to generation.*

***51** He hath shewed strength with his arm; he hath scattered the proud in the imagination of their hearts.*

***52** He hath put down the mighty from their seats, and exalted them of low degree.*

***53** He hath filled the hungry with good things; and the rich he hath sent empty away.*

***54** He hath helped his servant Israel, in remembrance of his mercy;*

***55** As he spake to our fathers, to Abraham, and to his seed forever.*

***56** And Mary abode with her about three months, and returned to her own house.*

Thanks be to God that Mary partnered with God. Today, we enjoy the fruit of that partnership. I declare to you today that partnership is the way out of tough times. Partner with Jesus today and the rest will be history. Jesus is the only One that can bring you out of every tough time. He is the solution, the answer, and the way out of every difficult time, deadly situation, and problem.

I want you to answer His call of partnership today and be blessed, and you will forever overcome your tough times.

Matthew 11:28-30 reads,

28 Come unto me, all ye that labour and are heavy laden, and I will give you rest.

29 Take my yoke upon you, and learn of me; for I am meek and lowly in heart: and ye shall find rest unto your souls.

30 For my yoke is easy, and my burden is light.

Partner with Jesus today and be blessed eternally!

Chapter 10

SECRET #4
FAITH

Faith is the fourth secret to overcoming your problems and your tough times. Nothing leaves heaven to earth without faith. Nothing leaves earth to heaven without faith.

FAITH IS DEFINED AS THE UNSHAKABLE CONFIDENCE IN GOD'S ABILITY.

Nobody can walk with God or man without faith. God told Joseph that for Egypt to overcome their tough times, they must have faith in His plan for them. Nothing good would happen if they failed to trust His plans. There are people today that have no faith in God's plan for their destiny. They trust man more than God. The Bible declares that without faith it is impossible to please God or ever be pleasing to Him.

Hebrews 11:6 reads,

But without faith it is impossible to please him: for he that cometh to God must believe that he is, and that he is a rewarder of them that diligently seek him.

Mark 11:22 reads,

And Jesus answering saith unto them, Have faith in God.

Faith is the currency of heaven. Faith is the language of God and heaven. Our God is a God of FAITH.

Faith is your only guarantee for victory in tough times. God commanded us to do the following by faith.

- Saved by faith
- Live by faith
- Walk by faith
- Speak by faith
- Fight the fight of faith
- Giving by faith
- Righteousness by faith

- Forgive by faith
- Love by faith
- Quench all darts by faith
- Rapture by faith
- God's children by faith

Knowing God and His ways, nothing works without faith.

NO FAITH, NO FUTURE

Romans 1:16-17 reads,

[16] ***For I am not ashamed of the gospel of Christ: for it is the power of God unto salvation to every one that believeth; to the Jew first, and also to the Greek.***

[17] ***For therein is the righteousness of God revealed from faith to faith: as it is written, The just shall live by faith.***

Hebrews 11:22-40 reads,

[22] ***By faith Joseph, when he died, made mention of the departing of the children of Israel; and gave commandment concerning his bones.***

23 By faith Moses, when he was born, was hid three months of his parents, because they saw he was a proper child; and they were not afraid of the king's commandment.

24 By faith Moses, when he was come to years, refused to be called the son of Pharaoh's daughter;

25 Choosing rather to suffer affliction with the people of God, than to enjoy the pleasures of sin for a season;

26 Esteeming the reproach of Christ greater riches than the treasures in Egypt: for he had respect unto the recompence of the reward.

27 By faith he forsook Egypt, not fearing the wrath of the king: for he endured, as seeing him who is invisible.

28 Through faith he kept the passover, and the sprinkling of blood, lest he that destroyed the firstborn should touch them.

29 By faith they passed through the Red sea as by dry land: which the Egyptians assaying to do were drowned.

30 By faith the walls of Jericho fell down, after they were compassed about seven days.

31 By faith the harlot Rahab perished not with them that believed not, when she had received the spies with peace.

32 And what shall I more say? for the time would fail me to tell of Gedeon, and of Barak, and of Samson, and of Jephthae; of David also, and Samuel, and of the prophets:

33 Who through faith subdued kingdoms, wrought righteousness, obtained promises, stopped the mouths of lions.

34 Quenched the violence of fire, escaped the edge of the sword, out of weakness were made strong, waxed valiant in fight, turned to flight the armies of the aliens.

35 Women received their dead raised to life again: and others were tortured, not accepting deliverance; that they might obtain a better resurrection:

36 And others had trial of cruel mockings and scourging's, yea, moreover of bonds and imprisonment:

37 They were stoned, they were sawn asunder, were tempted, were slain with the sword: they wandered about in sheepskins and goatskins; being destitute, afflicted, tormented;

38 (Of whom the world was not worthy:) they wandered in deserts, and in mountains, and in dens and caves of the earth.

[39] And these all, having obtained a good report through faith, received not the promise:

[40] God having provided some better thing for us, that they without us should not be made perfect.

Ephesians 6:16 reads,

Above all, taking the shield of faith, wherewith ye shall be able to quench all the fiery darts of the wicked.

1 Corinthians 2:5 reads,

That your faith should not stand in the wisdom of men, but in the power of God.

Build your faith and overcome all tough times. Faith is your only way of victory and the only way faith comes is through the Word of God.

Romans 10:17 reads,

So then faith cometh by hearing, and hearing by the word of God.

Remember, the Bible says according to your faith, be it unto you. Put your faith in God and Jesus today.

1 John 5:4-5 reads,

[4] For whatsoever is born of God overcometh the world: and this is the victory that overcometh the world, even our faith.

[5] Who is he that overcometh the world, but he that believeth that Jesus is the Son of God?

JESUS IS THE DELIVERER AND SAVIOR OF MANKIND
FROM ALL PROBLEMS AND TOUGH TIMES.
BELIEVE HIM TODAY AND BE FREE ETERNALLY.

Chapter 11

SECRET #5
CHANGE

Secret #5 is change, and change is powerful. God told Joseph to tell Pharaoh to make some changes in his life and government, and all will be well after seven years, if they obey God.

Genesis 41:38-44 reads,

> [38] ***And Pharaoh said unto his servants, Can we find such a one as this is, a man in whom the Spirit of God is?***
>
> [39] ***And Pharaoh said unto Joseph, Forasmuch as God hath shewed thee all this, there is none so discreet and wise as thou art:***

40 Thou shalt be over my house, and according unto thy word shall all my people be ruled: only in the throne will I be greater than thou.

41 And Pharaoh said unto Joseph, See, I have set thee over all the land of Egypt.

42 And Pharaoh took off his ring from his hand, and put it upon Joseph's hand, and arrayed him in vestures of fine linen, and put a gold chain about his neck;

43 And he made him to ride in the second chariot which he had; and they cried before him, Bow the knee: and he made him ruler over all the land of Egypt.

44 And Pharaoh said unto Joseph, I am Pharaoh, and without thee shall no man lift up his hand or foot in all the land of Egypt.

NO CHANGE, NO CHANCE

NO CHANGE, NO CREATIVITY

When people go through tough times, they never want to change, but tough times come to change them. In as much as people hate changes, yet it is the only thing that is constant. Look around you and see that everything is changing daily in technology. Inventions are changing, as companies and business are changing styles and methods.

The way to overcome and stay in the game is change. God has not changed but His methods change. You have to embrace the secret of change and change your life forever. Change will help you overcome your tough times.

As Pharaoh embraced change and overcame the famine and tough times, so must you change and things will change. Until you change, nothing changes. When Jesus came into this world, He came with a message of change. Repentance means change.

To see victory in your life, there are areas you must change. Let us look at a few.

AREAS TO CHANGE

- Change your heart.
- Change your thinking.
- Change your words.
- Change your habits.
- Change your strategies.
- Change your work/income.
- Change your choices.

- Change your decisions.
- Change your position.
- Change your focus.
- Change your plans.
- Change your environment.
- Change your team/associations.
- Change your actions/attitudes.
- Change your seed/giving.

EMBRACE CHANGE TODAY AND OVERCOME YOUR TOUGH TIMES.

The moment Pharaoh embraced change, the results followed almost immediately. He changed his leaders and replaced them with the right leader – Joseph. What do you need to change today? Do that now, do not delay. You will witness an amazing victory forever!

Chapter 12

SECRET #6 OBEDIENCE

OBEY THE LAWS!

The sixth secret is Obedience. It is the greatest demand that God requests from mankind. God loves to be obeyed more than anything else. Obedience is doing exactly what God says, when He says it, and the way He says it without delay or distractions. Delayed obedience is known to be disobedience. God told Joseph if Egypt was to overcome their tough times, they must obey all that He told them to the letter. Pharaoh did exactly what the Lord revealed, and they preserved the nation from deadly destruction and tough times.

Genesis 41:45-53 reads,

45 And Pharaoh called Joseph's name Zaphnathpaaneah; and he gave him to wife Asenath the daughter of Potipherah priest of On. And Joseph went out over all the land of Egypt.

46 And Joseph was thirty years old when he stood before Pharaoh king of Egypt. And Joseph went out from the presence of Pharaoh, and went throughout all the land of Egypt.

47 And in the seven plenteous years the earth brought forth by handfuls.

48 And he gathered up all the food of the seven years, which were in the land of Egypt, and laid up the food in the cities: the food of the field, which was round about every city, laid he up in the same.

49 And Joseph gathered corn as the sand of the sea, very much, until he left numbering; for it was without number.

50 And unto Joseph were born two sons before the years of famine came, which Asenath the daughter of Potipherah priest of On bare unto him.

*[51] **And Joseph called the name of the firstborn Manasseh: For God, said he, hath made me forget all my toil, and all my father's house.***

*[52] **And the name of the second called he Ephraim: For God hath caused me to be fruitful in the land of my affliction.***

*[53] **And the seven years of plenteousness, that was in the land of Egypt, were ended.***

Because Pharaoh and Joseph obeyed God, today we can learn and benefit from their obedience. They overcame the worst and the deadliest famine and recession ever. The cure for today's suffering, recession, and tough times is obedience to God. Obeying exactly what God is saying, taking these secrets, and applying them to your life. Do not just read or study them, but obey and do them. Everything God showed Pharaoh and Joseph, they did. They obeyed the instructions and direction of God. Your breakthrough is waiting for you at the other side of obedience.

OBEY GOD TODAY AND EXPERIENCE JOY

NO OBEDIENCE, NO OPEN DOORS OR HEAVENS

NO OBEDIENCE, NO OVERCOMING

The commandment of God today is still the same, it has not changed, and it will never change. Obey God today!

Jeremiah 7:23-24 reads,

[23] ***But this thing commanded I them, saying, Obey my voice, and I will be your God, and ye shall be my people: and walk ye in all the ways that I have commanded you, that it may be well unto you.***

[24] ***But they hearkened not, nor inclined their ear, but walked in the counsels and in the imagination of their evil heart, and went backward, and not forward.***

Jeremiah 11:1-8 reads,

1 The word that came to Jeremiah from the LORD saying,

[2] ***Hear ye the words of this covenant, and speak unto the men of Judah, and to the inhabitants of Jerusalem;***

[3] ***And say thou unto them, Thus saith the LORD God of Israel; Cursed be the man that obeyeth not the words of this covenant,***

[4] ***Which I commanded your fathers in the day that I brought them forth out of the land of Egypt, from the iron furnace, saying, Obey my voice, and do them, according to all which I command you: so shall ye be my people, and I will be your God:***

[5] That I may perform the oath which I have sworn unto your fathers, to give them a land flowing with milk and honey, as it is this day. Then answered I, and said, So be it, O LORD.

[6] Then the LORD said unto me, Proclaim all these words in the cities of Judah, and in the streets of Jerusalem, saying, Hear ye the words of this covenant, and do them.

[7] For I earnestly protested unto your fathers in the day that I brought them up out of the land of Egypt, even unto this day, rising early and protesting, saying, Obey my voice.

[8] Yet they obeyed not, nor inclined their ear, but walked everyone in the imagination of their evil heart: therefore I will bring upon them all the words of this covenant, which I commanded them to do: but they did them not.

God has spoken repeatedly, that obedience is all He requires and demands. To succeed you must obey.

Isaiah 1:18-19 reads,

[18] Come now, and let us reason together, saith the LORD: though your sins be as scarlet, they shall be as white as snow; though they be red like crimson, they shall be as wool.

[19] If ye be willing and obedient, ye shall eat the good of the land

To eat the good and the best of the land, we must walk in obedience to His voice today. There are certain things that are precious to God and in these, He demands total obedience to His voice today. There are certain things that are precious to God and in these, He demands total obedience without compromise. Let us look at a few of them; they will help you.

12 THINGS TO OBEY

1) Obey God's Principles.
2) Obey God's Purpose.
3) Obey God's Plan.
4) Obey God's Will.
5) Obey God's Laws.
6) Obey God's Process.
7) Obey God's Priorities.
8) Obey God's Voice.
9) Obey God's Structure.
10) Obey God's Standard.
11) Obey God's System.
12) Obey God's Prophets/Leaders.

When Pharaoh obeyed God and his chosen leader, Joseph, their nation escaped the hunger and recession. They overcame the poverty and storm that other nations did not.

Jeremiah 5:4 reads,

[4] ***Therefore I said, Surely these are poor; they are foolish: for they know not the way of the LORD, nor the judgment of their God.***

Job 36:11-12 reads,

[11] ***If they obey and serve him, they shall spend their days in prosperity, and their years in pleasures.***

[12] ***But if they obey not, they shall perish by the sword, and they shall die without knowledge.***

OBEY GOD TODAY AND OVECOME ALL HELL

The condition here is still obedience. If they obey and serve Me (God), prosperity will be their portion, not tough times. In your test and trials, choose to obey God. Obey the Lord today and overcome tough times.

Chapter 13

SECRET #7
PROBLEM SOLVING/SERVICE

BECOME THE SOLUTION

Secret #7 to overcoming tough times is problem solving or service. Everybody tends to run away from tough times and problems, but tough people will always win. Applying this secret in your life will put all trials, storms, troubles, struggles, and tough times away from you for life. They will become a thing of the past. Embrace the solution today.

REMEMBER

YOUR BATTLE IS FOR A REASON AND FOR A SEASON

Ecclesiastes 3:1-2 reads,

3 To everything there is a season, and a time to every purpose under the heaven:

4 A time to be born, and a time to die; a time to plant, and a time to pluck up that which is planted.

God spoke to Pharaoh through Joseph in famine and tough times on what to do; they believed, obeyed Him, and overcame. Joseph did not run away from the trouble like many would have done, but rather remained to solve it.

The Bible said Joseph took the bull by the horn and confronted the tough times and storm confidently. With seven secrets in his heart and hand, he brought Egypt out of their tough times. Therefore, so will you come out today.In our times today, especially with the just concluded elections here in America, we see a major move of God in our times and history. We have witnessed a black man becoming the president of this nation,; everybody walking in unity and in agreement, and believing that all will be well. We pray and believe God that His will and only His perfect will for this nation shall surely come to pass. America is the hope of the world and God cares about this nation and all the nations of the world. Let us embrace the challenge, standing up with this secret and these trials and tough times will pass like all other storms.

If God gave Joseph the way out, you too have the secrets in your hand right now; therefore, faithfully and confidently confront your tough times, knowing you are a winner and an overcomer. Every tough time is an opportunity to move forward and to grow.

Join the millions of people applying the truths in the book and overcome your tough times today. Joseph stayed in tough times without quitting. He faced the situation with the power of God and won.

Genesis 41:45-57 reads,

54 And the seven years of dearth began to come, according as Joseph had said: and the dearth was in all lands; but in all the land of Egypt there was bread.

55 And when all the land of Egypt was famished, the people cried to Pharaoh for bread: and Pharaoh said unto all the Egyptians, Go unto Joseph; what he saith to you, do.

[56] And the famine was over all the face of the earth: and Joseph opened all the storehouses, and sold unto the Egyptians; and the famine waxed sore in the land of Egypt.

[57] And all countries came into Egypt to Joseph for to buy corn; because that the famine was so sore in all lands.

Did you see that? Read that again, especially verse 57. The Bible said that all the nations of the world came to Joseph in Egypt to buy corn, because there were tough times and famine in all the face of the earth. Joseph became the solution; he solved the problem rather than running away with fear, unbelief or doubt. He stayed to serve and solve the problems in the land.

Everywhere you go, no matter what you face and go through, God placed you there to be the solution. Give the best of your service and watch God bless you.

Ecclesiastes 9:10

[10] Whatsoever thy hand findeth to do, do it with thy might; for there is no work, nor device, nor knowledge, nor wisdom, in the grave, whither thou goest.

1 Corinthians 15:57-58

[57] ***But thanks be to God, which giveth us the victory through our Lord Jesus Christ.***

[58] ***Therefore, my beloved brethren, be ye stedfast, unmoveable, always abounding in the work of the Lord, forasmuch as ye know that your labour is not in vain in the Lord.***

The Bible is clear on tough times and solutions. From Genesis to Revelation, we see problems and problem solvers. All the great names of the Bible solved problems; they all confronted Satan and suffering in God's name and defeated their tough times. This is God's plan for you.

Remember, no matter the tough times you are going through, it will not last. God's people will always overcome tough times. Please do not give up; you are a winner!

A LIST OF SOME OF THE PROBLEM SOLVERS IN THE BIBLE

- Noah
- Abraham
- Moses
- Deborah

- Ruth
- Elijah
- Elisha
- Esther
- Isaiah
- Jeremiah
- Daniel
- Nehemiah
- Hosea
- Jonah
- Jesus Christ of Nazareth
- Mary, the mother of Jesus
- Paul the Apostle
- Philip
- Dorcas
- Phebe, Paul's assistant
- And many others in Romans 16

You can add your name to the list of problem solvers. Join these brave people who never ran away from tough times but defeated them. Like Joseph, problem solvers never quit. In the name of Jesus you are an overcomer. Never ever quit or give up!

There are five qualities of all problem solvers:

1. Sacrifice – time, talent, treasure
2. Service – God and humanity
3. Sharing – gifts and talents
4. Seed sowing – good deeds

Saving lives – all the time

God wants you to stay and fight:

- Stay and save the marriage.
- Stay and save the ministry.
- Stay and save the mission.
- Stay and save the mandate.
- Stay and save mankind.
- Stay and save the corporation.
- Stay and save the business.
- Stay and save the school.
- Stay and save the hospital.
- Stay and save the nation.

Joseph stayed and saved the day and the entire nation.

Proverbs 24:10 reads,

[10] ***If thou faint in the day of adversity, thy strength is small.***

Galatians 6:9 reads,

[9] **And let us not be weary in well doing: for in due season we shall reap, if we faint not.**

1 Corinthians 4:17-18 reads,

[17] ***For this cause have I sent unto you Timotheus, who is my beloved son, and faithful in the Lord, who shall bring you into remembrance of my ways which be in Christ, as I teach every where in every church.***

[18] ***Now some are puffed up, as though I would not come to you.***

Paul faced all kinds of tough times and trials, but he confronted them all and won in the name of Jesus.

1 Corinthians 4:8-10 reads,

[8] ***Now ye are full, now ye are rich, ye have reigned as kings without us: and I would to God ye did reign, that we also might reign with you.***

[9] For I think that God hath set forth us the apostles last, as it were appointed to death: for we are made a spectacle unto the world, and to angels, and to men.

[10] We are fools for Christ's sake, but ye are wise in Christ; we are weak, but ye are strong; ye are honourable, but we are despised.

My friend, it is a new day for you! God is renewing your strength. With this secret in your hand, you will never know defeat anymore. Arise and fight in Jesus' name. Remember, tough times never last but God's people do.

Romans 8:35-39 reads,

[35] Who shall separate us from the love of Christ? shall tribulation, or distress, or persecution, or famine, or nakedness, or peril, or sword?

[36] As it is written, For thy sake we are killed all the day long; we are accounted as sheep for the slaughter.

[37] Nay, in all these things we are more than conquerors through him that loved us.

[38] For I am persuaded, that neither death, nor life, nor angels, nor principalities, nor powers, nor things present, nor things to come,

39 Nor height, nor depth, nor any other creature, shall be able to separate us from the love of God, which is in Christ Jesus our Lord.

Nothing can separate us from the love and plan of God. Follow the example of Joseph, a type of Jesus Christ, and obey the plan of God today. You are a problem solver. You are the solution to your generation. Rise up today. Rise in Jesus' name, rise in His strength. You can do it. Go in Jesus' name. Nothing can stop you now. No weapon fashioned against you will ever prosper. With this secret, tough times are gone forever. Make God proud. Solve the problem today in His name. Serve Him the best you can.

There are five reasons people run from giants and tough times. It is worth mentioning them.

- Ignorance – Don't be ignorant anymore.
- Immaturity – Don't be immature anymore.
- Instability – Don't be unstable anymore.
- Impatience – Don't be impatient anymore.
- Insecurity – Don't be insecure anymore.

You now have the same secrets that Joseph was empowered with and used in your hands. Move to action now. I will surely see you at the top. There is no stopping now. Move on. These secrets brought me to where I am today, and they are taking me into my future and destiny. Rapture is my limit. We are taking territories and nations for Jesus Christ. Join the army of problem solvers and world savers today.

Chapter 14

NEVER GIVE UP

Tough times never last; I say that to you again, tough times never last. From the entire Bible stories, we have studied and read none of the tough times, troubles, trials, storms, floods, wars or calamities lasted forever. They all passed.

Whatever you are going through right now, while reading this book, did not come to remain or take you out, but to bring you into another dimension. You are more than a conqueror. Like Joseph, believe God and His words. Trust Him and know He will never fail you. God promised to help you and see you through. Practice every secret daily and read the book again and again. You can always go back to check how you are doing, and what you are missing out and correct it.

Meditate on the following scriptures for the next 30 days:

Psalm 54:4 reads,

4 Behold, God is mine helper: the Lord is with them that uphold my soul.

Isaiah 50:4 reads,

4 The Lord GOD hath given me the tongue of the learned, that I should know how to speak a word in season to him that is weary: he wakeneth morning by morning, he wakeneth mine ear to hear as the learned.

Isaiah 50:7-10 reads,

7 For the Lord GOD will help me; therefore shall I not be confounded: therefore have I set my face like a flint, and I know that I shall not be ashamed.

8 He is near that justifieth me; who will contend with me? let us stand together: who is mine adversary? let him come near to me.

9 Behold, the Lord GOD will help me; who is he that shall condemn me? lo, they all shall wax old as a garment; the moth shall eat them up.

[10] Who is among you that feareth the LORD, that obeyeth the voice of his servant, that walketh in darkness, and hath no light? let him trust in the name of the LORD, and stay upon his God.

Romans 10:11-13 reads,

[11] For the scripture saith, Whosoever believeth on him shall not be ashamed.

[12] For there is no difference between the Jew and the Greek: for the same Lord over all is rich unto all that call upon him.

[13] For whosoever shall call upon the name of the Lord shall be saved.

REMEMBER YOU ARE AN OVERCOMER;
NEVER GIVE UP BECAUSE TOUGH TIMES NEVER LAST.
REMAIN BLESSED!

Chapter 15

NOW, OVERCOME TOUGH TIMES

All has been said, truths have been revealed, and secrets have been given; now go and overcome. Like Joseph, take dominion over all tough times and remember Jesus said, "Be of good cheer, I have overcome the world" (John 16:33).

Begin to practice these seven secrets right away; do not wait another minute. Remember, failure to plan is planning to fail. Plan your escape now. Do the impossible and unbelievable; start immediately, begin today and you will see great results. Devotedly and sincerely with conviction, follow each secret and step outlined in this book, and watch God change things.

Your daily habits and routine are a sure way to know what you really believe. Take small steps slowly, but surely every day and you will conquer every debt, divorce, danger, and devil. Take dominion today.

Write to me; send me your praise report, prayer request or questions. God wants to use me to help you. Remember, tough times never last; do not give up!

Chapter 16

MY STORY FOR HIS GLORY

My many thanks and praise go to Almighty God, my Father; to my Savior and Lord, Jesus Christ, and to my best friend, Helper, Mentor, and Teacher – the Holy Spirit for giving me these secrets for my generation. This is especially timely now that we are presently facing a very crucial time in our country, America. The global crisis and economic failures around the world today call for action and intervention from those individuals that God will work through.

I am humbled to be a part of this end-time army of problem solvers. Everything God created was created to solve problems. Time will not permit me to write everything I have been through in my life. There will not be enough space to write them all until eternity, but God is faithful, He has seen me through each one together with my family.

Just last year, when my father passed on to glory in his sleep, my shock was comforted by Jesus Christ. In the same year, five of my best friends also went home to be with the Lord. It was one attack after another. However, like Jesus said, "I will build my Church and the gates of hell shall not prevail;" I know that the gates of hell cannot and will not prevail in my life in Jesus' name. My faith is stronger and I know that at the name of Jesus, every knee has bowed. It is well.

Chapter 17

HOW YOU CAN KNOW GOD'S LOVE

My dear friend, though I mentioned throughout this book that tough times will never last, without a relationship with God through Jesus Christ, tough times can last. There is a God in Heaven who loves you as you are and not as you should be. The heart of the human being longs for God, and logic demands divine existence. While everyone believes God is, most people sense separation from God. We know God must be holy and good. We see ourselves as unholy and not good. We conclude, therefore, that God is angry with us, and we cannot know him.

The good news is that God loves us as we are. That love will save us from our sin and make us what we should be as God's children. God loves you and wants your tough times to end today. Please take a few minutes to read how you can have a relationship with God, experience the love of God, and have your tough times end.

John 3:16 reads,

"For God so loved the world, that He gave His only begotten Son, that whosoever believeth in Him should not perish, but have everlasting life."

We hear Jesus say, "God so loved the world." God's love has no limitations. He loves "so" much more than we can imagine. He loves everyone – not just some.

Romans 5:8 tells us that God loved us so much that, "while we were yet sinners, Christ died for us."

Romans 3:23 reads,

For all have sinned and come short of the glory of God.

This verse tells us that all people have sinned. We have fallen short of God's intended purpose for us. God made us to know Him, to receive His love, and to love Him in return.

For love to be love, for God to be God, and for humans to be humans, God gave us a choice. We can choose to love ourselves and turn to our selfish pursuits, but that is sin. In our sin we cannot know God and His love. The result of sin is that we are lost, which means being separated from God.

Romans 6:23 reads,

For the wages of sin is death; but the gift of God is eternal life through Christ Jesus or Lord.

Wages are just payment, due reward or what one has coming because of labor. The just payment for our sin is death.

Death here means spiritual insensitivity. When we are still in our sin, we have no life with God. We are alive physically but dead spiritually. If we continue in that condition, we will be separated from God for all eternity.

The wages of sin is death, but God's free gift is eternal life. While wages are earned, a gift is offered with no strings attached. God says He will give us eternal life – life with Him – in the place of sin's payment of death.

How can God remain true to His holiness and forgive unholy sinners? It is because Jesus, His son, has paid the price for sin by His death on the cross.

2 Corinthians 5:21 says, "*For he hath made him to be sin for us, who knew no sin; that we might be made the righteousness of God in him.*"

Jesus arose from the grave to conquer sin and death for all who receive Him as God's free gift.

How can you receive God's free gift of love and life?

Read Romans 10:9-10.

A person receives God's free gift of love and life by placing faith in Jesus Christ. To believe is simply to take God at His word. With our whole heart, we believe that Jesus is God's Son who died for our sins on the cross and arose from the grave after three days to live in us as Savior and Lord.

To believe in Jesus will result in confessing that faith with one's mouth.

- *Do you acknowledge that you are a sinner?*
- *Do you believe by faith that Jesus, God's Son, died for your sin on the cross?*
- *Will you now confess Him as your Savior and Lord?*

Romans 10:13 reads,

For whosoever shall call upon the name of the Lord shall be saved.

This verse says that any person who calls upon the name of Jesus, the Lord, shall be saved. To call means simply to ask in prayer. The verse does not require one to know more, do better, clean up one's life, or in any way try to add to what Jesus has done for us.

Will you now call upon Jesus to save you from your sin so that you can know God's love and forgiveness?

SAY THIS PRAYER:

"Dear God, I confess that I am a sinner, and I am sorry. I need a Savior. I know I cannot save myself. I believe by faith that Jesus, Your Son, died on the cross for my sins. I believe He arose from the grave to live as my Lord. I turn from my sin. I ask You, Lord Jesus, to forgive my sin and come into my heart. I trust you as my Savior and receive you as my Lord. Thank you, Jesus for saving me."

When anyone calls on the Lord in this manner, that person is saved according to God's Word. If you pray a prayer of repentance and faith, you are saved. You have God's word on it. Believe in Him.

WELCOME TO GOD'S FAMILY!

Now, as a way to grow closer to God, the Bible tells us to follow up on our commitment.

- Find a local church where you can worship God.
- Get baptized as commanded by Christ.
- Tell someone else about your new faith in Christ.
- Spend time with God each day. It does not have to be a long period of time. Just develop the daily habit of praying to Him and reading His Word.
- Ask God to increase your faith and your understanding of the Bible.
- Read the gospel of John in the Bible to find out what God says about Jesus, about you, and about being born again.
- Seek fellowship with other followers of Jesus.
- Develop a group of believing friends to answer your questions and support you.

Congratulations on your decision. I rejoice with you, but most importantly, heaven is rejoicing with you. The Bible tells us that heaven rejoices over one sinner that comes to Christ.

Luke 15:7 and 10 reads,

7 I say unto you, that likewise joy shall be in heaven over one sinner that repenteth, more than over ninety and nine just persons, which need no repentance.

10 Likewise, I say unto you, there is joy in the presence of the angels of God over one sinner that repenteth.

God bless you!

BISHOP DR. EMMANUEL MACJONES

THE SOLUTION CENTER

Welcome to the solution Center! You will find a summarized list of other recommended life changing materials produced by EMJ Ministries and Bishop Emmanuel Macjones.

Books

1) Making Money God's Way
2) The Anger of God
3) One Day
4) The Covenant of Protection
5) The Covenant of Blessing
6) The Overcomer
7) Why Men Do Not Have Money
8) Press On
9) Understanding the Help of The Holy Spirit
10) I Will Arise

11) You Have What You Say
12) The Power of Unity
13) 26 Ways to Change Your Life Forever
14) The Power and Benefits of Fasting

Audio Messages on CD:

1) The Foundation for Success
2) The Work of the Believer
3) Love the Greatest Achievement
4) The Power of Relationships
5) The Plan of God for Relationships Part 1&2
6) The Importance of Relationships
7) How to Make Your Relationship Heaven on Earth
8) Don't Be Afraid (Series)
9) The Power of the Word (Series)
10) Don't be a Foolish Christian
11) How not to be a Foolish Christian
12) The Danger of Pride
13) The Power of Love (Series)
14) The Mission of Jesus
15) The Power of Vision
16) Depending on the Word of God
17) Eight Secrets to Success

18) The Eight Enemies of Success
19) The Wonders of God
20) How to Release the Wonders of God
21) Operating Under the Spirit of Christ
22) What To Do When You Don't Know What Else To Do (Series)
23) Developing the Habit of Finishing Well
24) Tough Times Never Last (Series)
25) Praying Successfully
26) Three Things to Do To Constantly Experience Miracles
27) Born to Win
28) How to Win
29) How to Win the War against Satanic Attack
30) Depending on the Help of God (Series)

For further spiritual assistance, contact

EMJ MINISTRIES

Postal Address:

10125 Colesville RD

Suite 3157 Silver Spring,

MD 20901

Tel: (703) 898 2111 or (202) 697-1408

E-Mail: info@overcomerschurch.org

bishopmacjones@gmail.com

ABOUT THE AUTHOR

BISHOP DR. EMMANUEL MACJONES

Bishop Dr. Emmanuel MacJones is one of today's most dynamic and encouraging leaders. His enthusiasm for the Lord is truly inspiring. He is the founder and president of EMJ Ministries as well as the presiding Bishop of God Pleasers Family Church Worldwide, non-denominational ministries, with branches and centers in London, USA, Israel, Germany, and Africa.

Dr. MacJones remains one of the most sought after speakers, with over twenty-eight years of experience in ministry. He encourages people to stay focused on what matters most – their relationship with God, family, people, the Kingdom, and fulfillment in life. He inspires individuals to live a life of purpose, a life of an over comer, and of pleasing God. He has authored other best-selling books, among which are "I Will Arise," "Making Money God's Way," "Understanding The Help of The Holy Spirit," and "The Power and Benefits of Fasting."

He is married to Bishop Mrs. Mercy Mac Jones and they are blessed with five children. Dr. Macjones is currently based in Maryland, USA.

CPSIA information can be obtained at www.ICGtesting.com
Printed in the USA
BVOW08s2208160816

459233BV00001B/1/P